THE
STIR FRY
COOK

In the same series

Chinese Cookery Secrets
The Curry Secret
Authentic Indian Cookery

Uniform with this book

The photograph on the front cover shows Mandarin Prawns (page 33). Photograph taken by Paul Noble, Burgess Hill, West Sussex.

THE
STIR FRY
COOK

Caroline Young

RIGHT WAY

CONTENTS

INTRODUCTION

Sometimes I feel my whole life revolves around food! Whether exploring new eating habits, developing recipes, trying out new cookware or appliances, feeding my family or keeping an eye on what's new in the supermarkets – it's an enormous, fascinating subject and one I would love to encourage you to learn more about.

Perhaps it is time we made food more important. By that I don't mean eating more of it or spending more money on it but making it a more important part of our daily life. Even on a strict budget, cooking can be a great pleasure – a way of showing affection and appreciation to family, friends and yourself.

Treat food with the respect it deserves. Food is related to history, climate, geography and economics. Take time to find out where foods come from, how they are eaten in their native habitat, how to choose good food and how to cook it with care – and pleasure.

Long ago my family became resigned to part of our holidays being a tour of the supermarkets, food and cookware shops wherever we happened to be. Strange foods, cookery books and unfamiliar cooking pots became our holiday souvenirs.

Many of the recipes in this book are the results of those holidays. All the recipes are cooked in one pan – a frypan or a wok and take less than thirty minutes to prepare and cook. The ingredients given are for two servings but are easy to double up to serve four – remember you will need a bigger frypan. Each chapter has very simple, inexpensive recipes as well as one or two more elaborate-looking dishes for those times when you want to make a good impression! Follow every step as I have described it and you will find each recipe very easy to complete. However, remember a recipe is only a starting point – when you feel happy with my choice of ingredients, try using a different fish from the one I have suggested or try swapping courgettes for broccoli. Be adventurous and enjoy making a dish unique to you! That is what a good cookbook should do – inspire you to experiment and develop your own ideas.

Both metric and imperial measurements are given in the recipes. However, you should use only one set of measurements when following a recipe and not mix the two. The spoon measurements used are level.

The following abbreviations are used:

tsp = teaspoon
tbsp = tablespoon
pt = pint
mins. = minutes
fl oz = fluid ounces

I hope you will enjoy using this book as much as I did writing it. Even more important – enjoy eating the end results!

1. PICK OF THE PANS

Whatever the job, having the right tools makes work much easier and far more enjoyable. This applies in the kitchen too. I have certain pans, knives and other tools that are old friends. They have travelled from house to house with me and are used almost daily. They have earned their place in my kitchen by being well made, easy to take care of and able to do the job successfully and effortlessly. Other pieces of equipment that haven't fulfilled these requirements find themselves sent to the nearest jumble sale very quickly! It takes time, and a few mistakes, to build up a basic set of kitchen equipment but once you have, they will serve you well for many years.

All the recipes in this book are cooked in one pan. This may be a frypan (either one that goes on the hob or an electric plug-in model) or a wok. You may well have one of these with which you are very happy. If not, may I guide you to choosing a pan suitable for the type of hob you have?

Let's look at **frypans** first. A good all-purpose sized pan should be at least 10 in/25cm in diameter and have a lid. Many of the recipes require the food to be covered at some point. This traps the steam, keeps the food moist and reduces the cooking time. (If your existing pan has no lid, you could improvise with a double thickness of cooking foil placed over the food and very carefully folded over the edges of the pan.)

The quality of the pan will be indicated by the price, and the better the quality, the longer the pan will last. The weight of the pan should feel comfortable to you, the cook. Remember, a cheap light-weight pan may get too hot, burn the food and eventually the base will become uneven. The choice of material includes very heavy enamelled cast-iron, aluminium and stainless steel.

Cast-iron pans are extremely good conductors of heat. If the food sticks to the base of the pan, reduce the temperature of the hob. They are suitable for gas, electric or solid hobs. If you have a ceramic or halogen hob, look for pans with specially coated bases to avoid scratching the hob. Always lift, not pull, pans off these hobs. Cast-iron pans may have non-stick finishes. Allow cast-iron pans to cool slightly after use, then wash in hot, soapy water. If food has stuck to the pan, leave to soak for a while. Use only nylon, plastic or wooden spoons or spatulas and pot scourers to avoid damaging the surfaces of pans both with and without non-stick surfaces. With good care they should last a lifetime.

Good quality *aluminium pans* (buy the heaviest gauge/weight you can afford) are also excellent conductors of heat. Reduce the temperature of the hob, if you find the food sticks to the base of the pan. Most aluminium pans have a non-stick finish. They are suitable for gas, electric and halogen hobs. For solid or ceramic hobs, choose an especially heavy-based pan. To clean an aluminium pan, allow it to cool slightly before washing in hot, soapy water. Use only nylon scourers.

Stainless steel is not a particularly good conductor of heat, so the best pans have a base of copper or aluminium sandwiched between the steel. Stainless steel retains the heat well, so when a recipe states 'reduce the heat', reduce it to very low. These pans are suitable for gas and electric hobs. For ceramic, halogen or solid hobs look for stainless steel pans especially designed for these hobs. To clean, slip a stainless steel pan into hot, soapy water immediately after use, rinse and dry. Stuck-on foods will loosen with soaking, then rub with a nylon scourer. Copper-based pans should not be immersed to soak, just fill with soapy water and leave to stand.

If you have one of the very new induction hobs, you must use pans specifically designed for them – check the labels.

Electric frypan. If you have very limited cooking facilities this could be a useful appliance. It is totally self-contained, simply needing a 13 amp. socket. The frypan has a detachable control switch which thermostatically determines the temperature of the pan's surface. It usually has a non-stick finish and a high lid enabling the frypan to be used for quite large foods such as a whole chicken. Although expensive it is very versatile.

Woks and stir fry pans. These are deeper than frypans and may have one long or two short handles. The traditional wok has a very rounded base which is very successful on gas hobs. For all other types of hob look for a wok with a flat bottom. Some woks are made of carbon steel. With these pans it is particularly important to read the manufacturer's handbook carefully with regard to any pre-seasoning the pan may need. It may have a protective coating on it which, if not removed, might taint the food. Follow their suggestions for cleaning and storage too, to ensure a long pan life. Other woks are made of aluminium and may have a non-stick interior and a coloured porcelain enamel exterior. Stir fry pans usually have a non-stick finish but no lid.

Just a word on non-stick finishes. These do vary in quality which is naturally reflected in the price. Treat them with care and they will last for years. Avoid using knives and rough-edged cooking tools in them as once a surface is scratched, it is weakened. A lightly scratched pan can continue to be used, though you may need to add oil. Once the surface has begun to peel, the pan should be discarded. Never use non-stick pans on a very high heat. After use, allow the pan to cool slightly before immersing in water. Wash in warm, soapy water, using only a soft brush or nylon scouring pad. Stacking other pans inside a non-stick pan will quickly result in scratching. Store upside down or with the lid on.

2. KITCHEN BASICS

To produce good food you don't need to have an elaborate kitchen filled with all the latest gadgets. All the recipes in this book need the minimum of kitchen equipment and can be cooked equally well in a bedsitter, a caravan or the family kitchen.

Established kitchens will have all the necessary tools but if you are just beginning to cook, these are the things I find indispensable.

Knives: please don't waste your money buying flimsy, cheap knives. Good quality knives, as well as performing well, will last for a very long time if you take care of them.

Essentials – a small vegetable knife with a pointed blade; a larger all-purpose knife with a blade about 6 in/15cm long for chopping and slicing; plus a knife sharpener.

Useful – a serrated-edged breadknife makes cutting bread easier and a small round-ended flexible palette knife is handy for spreading butter, etc. You can peel vegetables and fruit with the smaller knife but it is quicker and safer with an inexpensive swivel-type potato peeler.

Store knives either in a slotted block, on a magnetic rack or in a divided drawer so that they can't rub against one another and become blunt. Wash in hot, soapy water after use and also between using for cooked and raw foods. Wipe dry immediately after washing.

Cutting boards: essential is a medium-sized cutting board made of impervious heavy-duty plastic which does not absorb smells and bacteria. Wash in hot, soapy water. If it becomes stained, clean with a mild bleach solution and rinse well.

   Useful – a wooden bread board (which can double up as a cheese board).

Set of measuring spoons: essential for accurate measuring of oils, spices, etc.

1 pt/600ml measuring jug: essential for accurate liquid measures. If you can find the wider-topped version it will also come in handy as a small mixing bowl. Available in heat-proof glass or plastic.

Mixing bowls: one about 1 pt/600ml plus a larger one, either in heat-proof glass or plastic. Will also double up as salad or fruit bowls.

Colander or large strainer: for draining pasta, washing salad greens, etc. I find a colander easiest as it is self-supporting and I prefer the brightly coloured plastic ones to the metal variety as they are lighter, cheaper, don't go rusty or come apart, and are more attractive!

Tin opener: need I say more!

Garlic press: you can finely chop garlic with a sharp knife but it is quicker with a garlic press. Look for the type that comes apart for easier washing.

Grater: essential for grating cheese, lemon rind, making breadcrumbs, etc. Again the better quality type will virtually last for ever. I have one where the cheese, etc., grates into a box which also holds the blade steady.

Stainless steel wire whisk: not essential, a fork will do most jobs but a whisk is faster and more efficient.

Lemon squeezer: you can squeeze lemons or oranges with a firm hand but this tool is more efficient and separates the seeds from the juice! I have a very cheap one where the squeezer part sits on top of its own jug.

Spatulas: also called fish slices. These are large straight-ended tools used for lifting chops, etc., from the frypan; also for stirring foods when cooking. If your frypan has a non-stick finish, you must use a spatula suitable for such a surface or you will damage the pan. I use very smooth wooden spatulas for this. (If a new wooden spatula feels rough along the edge, smooth with fine sandpaper before use.)

Spoons: essential is one large metal or heatproof plastic spoon for serving foods. A slotted (perforated) spoon is useful for lifting certain foods out of the pan but leaving any fat or liquid still in the pan, e.g. when crisping bacon. I also like to have one or two wooden spoons as well; two can also double for tossing and serving green salads.

Vegetable scrubber: or a sturdy nail brush. For scrubbing rather than peeling root vegetables.

Kitchen scissors: not essential but very handy.

Kitchen scales: with the majority of the ingredients in the recipes in this book, very accurate weighing is not essential and a little more or less will not be disastrous. There are one or two situations however, where the balance of two ingredients is important. For instance, in all the recipes using uncooked rice, it is essential to have the correct amount of rice in proportion to the amount of liquid. Being a dried food, rice needs a specific amount of liquid to become edible. Too little rice in proportion to liquid, the end result will be soupy. Too much and the dish will be stodgy, so weighing the rice is important.

The price of kitchen scales varies enormously so shop around. Choose one with easy-to-read measurements and a good sized bowl or tray to hold the food. Like so many things for the kitchen, buy a good set of scales, take care of them and they will last for years.

Salt and pepper mills: to me these are essential as I far prefer the flavour of freshly milled coarse sea salt and black peppercorns to that of salt and pepper sold ready ground. You can find several very inexpensive mills already packed with salt or pepper, which can be refilled. Keep them away from steam to avoid the contents becoming damp.

3. FOOD FACTS

No matter where we shop, be it in an enormous supermarket, specialist food shop, the local corner store or in the street markets, the sheer quantity and variety of food on offer today is bewildering and enormous. It can be confusing wondering how to choose foods, whether they should be kept in the refrigerator or a cupboard and finally, how to cook them. The following list of ingredients used in this book is to help you find some of the lesser known foods, and gives details on how to store and use them, with useful information on the safe storage of food in general.

CREAMED COCONUT
Blocks of creamed coconut can usually be found among the dried fruits, nuts and baking ingredients in supermarkets or in Indian food shops. Once opened it will keep for some time tightly wrapped in the fridge. Just a small amount adds a subtle rich flavour and texture to a dish such as a curry.

CREAMS, FROMAGE FRAIS AND YOGHURTS
I very rarely use cream simply spooned or poured over food so do not feel the least bit guilty when I use it in cooking. Even just a spoonful stirred into a dish improves

the texture and flavour. The simplest and most delicious sauce of all is made by pouring a small carton of double cream into the pan after cooking chicken, meat or fish in it, and allowing the cream to bubble until hot. Single cream will enrich a dish but also make a sauce thinner, while double cream (with a higher fat content) will thicken when heated.

Fromage frais (also called fromage blanc) may be very low fat (1%) or enriched with a little cream (8%), but even the latter still has a lower fat content than single cream. The very low fat variety needs stabilising before heating by stirring in 1 tsp (5ml) cornflour to ¼ pt (150ml), otherwise it will separate. The 8% is more stable but do not overheat it.

Yoghurts also come with varying fat contents from the very low fat (less than 0.5% fat) through to the very creamy Greek-style yoghurt. Like fromage frais, the lower fat varieties need to be stabilised (see above) before use in hot dishes. For best results allow yoghurt to come to room temperature before adding to hot ingredients.

Always buy these dairy products in small quantities, keep covered, well chilled and use quickly.

CORNFLOUR
Cornflour is a very white, very fine flour ground from wheat kernels. It is used to thicken sauces and to coat foods before cooking, especially in oriental dishes. Before adding to hot foods to thicken a dish, it must always be mixed to a smooth cream with a little cold water. Stir into the sauce and bring just to the boil, stirring constantly, until thickened and smooth.

FATS AND OILS
Setting aside the health argument regarding fats and oils, using too generous an amount of either can actually spoil a recipe, making it taste too greasy and masking the flavours of the other ingredients. Far better is to use a small measured amount of the fat or oil most suitable for that recipe.

I prefer to use a good, unsalted, block butter when the flavour will add to the overall result, particularly when cooking fish or fruit dishes. Buy butter frequently in small quantities rather than in bulk and always keep well wrapped in the refrigerator, well away from strong-smelling foods. A good quality block margarine could be substituted but may alter the final flavour of the dish. Soft tub butters and margarines have water added to them. They may spit when heated.

For foods with a more robust flavour such as peppers, garlic and onions, I choose an olive oil. The range of colour and flavour found in olive oils depends on where the olives were grown and which pressing of the fruit was used. Top of the range is 'extra virgin' olive oil with a superb rich flavour, aroma and depth of colour. Olive oil labelled 'pure' is probably a blend of subsequent press-ings. Shop around and find the one (or two) that you prefer, using pure olive oil for cooking and virgin olive oil for the rich flavour. Olive oil is a mono-saturated fat and is now considered good for the heart but, if wished, another good quality vegetable oil may be substituted. The flavour won't be the same though!

Specialist oils such as walnut, sesame and hazelnut are usually used as flavourings not cooking oils. Sprinkle onto cooked dishes such as stir frys just before serving or use in salad dressings.

Store oils in a cool, dark place, not in the fridge.

GARLIC

I find most people either adore garlic or absolutely hate it – I have to admit I am one of the former and so use garlic liberally in my cooking. It is one of the basic 'flavouring' vegetables together with onions and celery. If you don't share my enthusiasm for a strong garlic flavour, heat the peeled garlic clove in the oil or butter and then remove before adding other ingredients. The flavour is also lessened if the centre of the garlic clove is removed before crushing. Halve the clove lengthwise and lift out and discard the pale green or yellow centre.

Buy garlic bulbs that are firm with a dry, papery skin. Store in a cool, airy place such as a bowl. Do not keep in a plastic bag or the fridge. Discard any bulbs that have started to sprout.

I don't like the flavours you get from garlic powder or

salt but have found the tubes or jars of garlic purée acceptable.

GINGER

The strange knobbly roots of fresh ginger are now available in most supermarkets and greengrocers. Buy in small amounts – you can just snap off a piece the size you want. To use, cut off the brown peel and either grate or finely chop the creamy-yellow, fibrous flesh. Cooking releases the warm, mild flavour. Any unused root may be kept well wrapped in the fridge for a few days.

HERBS

A wide selection of fresh herbs is now available in the shops nearly all the year. For flavour and appearance, they are my first choice. Buy in small quantities, keep in the fridge and use quickly. Why not try growing a pot of parsley or chives all the year round on the kitchen window-sill? Even I, with very ungreen fingers, manage to keep a good supply that way. However, when the very herb I particularly want isn't around, I prefer to use freeze-dried herbs rather than the conventional dried variety. Again buy in small quantities, keep in screw-topped jars and use quickly before they lose their flavour.

HONEY

Honey adds a very mellow flavour to both sweet and savoury dishes. Buy the clear unset variety for cooking and keep in a cool place (not in the fridge). It may crystallize with age but will liquify when heated.

LEMON JUICE

Nothing can beat the crisp clean flavour of freshly squeezed lemon juice, but bottled juice (or the plastic lemon variety) will do in an emergency. Buy fresh lemons when required and use quickly before they go hard and dry. They may be stored in the fridge or in a cool cupboard. Always store bottled juice in the refrigerator after opening and make a note of the 'use-by' date. Stale juice will definitely spoil a recipe.

MUSTARDS
There are numerous varieties of mustards to choose from
but basically they can be divided into three types. The
original English mustard powder is very hot and a tiny
pinch in a recipe goes a long way, so use with caution. The
milder made-up mustards are either smooth such as the
Dijon or the darker Bordeaux type, or the whole-grain
type where the mustard seeds have been coarsely crushed.
A jar of each one is always in my cupboard. I like to add a
spoonful or so of both the made-up mustards to all kinds
of recipes. The smooth mustards add a warmth to
sauces, while the whole-grain type add flavour and
interesting texture.

Store tightly closed in a cool, dry cupboard and wipe the
tops of jars if they become encrusted with dried mustard.

PASTA
The variety of pasta available in our shops indicates just
how popular the staple dish of Italy has become, probably
due to the simplicity and speed of cooking. Either natural
or wholemeal pasta, fresh or dried, may be used.
Remember dried wholemeal pasta will need a longer
cooking time. Pasta 'verdi' has spinach purée added to
colour it. When cooking pasta on its own, before adding
to a recipe, adding 1 tsp/5ml of oil to the water will stop it
sticking together. Never cook pasta until it is very soft, it
should still have a slightly firm bite to it, described by the
Italians as 'al dente' ('to the tooth'). Always drain pasta
very thoroughly, particularly hollow shapes such as shells.
Shake the colander well to remove every drop of water, to
prevent diluting the rest of the recipe.

Chinese noodles are a great time-saver as they have
been pre-cooked by steaming. They only need to be
covered with boiling water and left to stand, covered,
while you put together the sauce. One or two varieties are
on the oriental food shelves in supermarkets but a visit to
an oriental supermarket will reveal numerous other kinds.

RICE
I am told there are about seven thousand varieties of rice
in the world so we have plenty of scope to experiment!
Brown 'whole-grain' rice still has its outer layer of bran,

which is valuable dietary fibre, but it needs longer cooking and possibly more liquid. White rice has been milled or 'polished' to remove the outer bran layer. Some 'white' rice has a pale gold or amber colour.

Savoury dishes use long or medium grain rice such as Patna or Basmati whose grains remain separate and fluffy, while short grain rice is used for puddings. The exception is the Italian Arborio rice, used for risottos, in which the short rice grains swell and hold together.

Wild rice is not actually a rice but the seed of a grass. It is very expensive but the exotic-looking, long, dark brown grains are now sold in reasonably priced packs mixed with long grain white rice. Well worth trying for a special meal.

Supermarkets stock a wide range of rices and rice mixes, though you may need to go to an Italian delicatessen for Arborio rice. Rice keeps almost indefinitely in a lidded container in a cool, dry cupboard so is worth buying in bulk.

I have recently added canned rice to my cupboard. It is already cooked and needs only the addition of a little liquid (to create steam) and heating through. I find it very useful in those recipes which require cooked rice to be added near the end of the cooking time.

SALT AND PEPPER

Like sugar, salt is a flavour enhancer and should be added with a very light hand. Always taste food before adding salt as other ingredients such as stock may already contain enough salt. I prefer to use the coarse sea salt which I grind in a mill exactly the same as for black peppercorns. Look for very inexpensive refillable mills where the salt and peppercorns are sold.

SPICES

Buy spices in very small amounts and store them in jars with tight-fitting lids to preserve their aroma. Once that has gone it is time to buy fresh ones.

SOY AND TAMARI SAUCE

Soy sauce is the familiar Chinese flavouring made from fermented soya beans. It is easily found either in a light version with a delicate flavour, or in the darker more salty version. Choose the flavour you prefer. Tamari is also made from soya beans but without any additives, including sugar. It has a slightly stronger flavour than soy sauce. Look for it in oriental food stores or healthfood shops.

STOCK CUBES

The strength of stock cubes varies considerably and you need to try different brands to find the one for you. Regardless of the type of meat I am using, for many dishes I frequently choose to use a vegetable stock cube as I like the light herby flavour. Vegetable stock cubes can also be used as a seasoning, just crumbling a cube into a recipe without dissolving it in water first. Keep stock cubes in a dry cupboard.

SUGARS

Sugar should not be thought of as an undesirable ingredient but as a seasoning. Just a little sugar brings out the natural flavours in other foods, and enriches and adds colour to recipes, such as when browning onions. Don't leave out the pinch of sugar specified in some recipes or you will spoil the end result.

TOFU

Tofu is bean curd made from soya beans and is very nutritious. It is a good source of protein yet has low fat content. Widely used in oriental and vegetarian cookery, tofu has a very unappealing appearance and bland taste. It needs to be marinated or used with strong flavours which it absorbs. It is also available in a smoked version. There are several types but these recipes use the set 'firm' version. Look for tofu on the chilled cheese shelves in supermarkets or chiller cabinets in oriental or healthfood stores. Don't be put off by the initial appearance and lack of flavour, it is well worth trying.

TOMATO PURÉE

This is a concentrated tomato paste with a much stronger flavour than tomato ketchup. Just a little will add a rich tomato flavour to a dish. It is sold in jars or tubes. The jars are economical but need to be used up quickly (store in the fridge once opened). Buy in tubes if you only use it rarely.

VEGETABLES
'Small is best' is my advice when buying vegetables.
Young vegetables have a higher moisture content than
when old so have more flavour, need less cooking liquid
and time. Buy in small quantities, store in a cool place
(not in plastic bags as these make vegetables sweat and so
go mouldy) and use quickly for optimum flavour and food
value. If possible I prefer to scrub rather than peel
vegetables. Use a very firm bristled nail brush or a special
vegetable brush. Mushrooms only need wiping with a
damp cloth. Avoid peeling if possible, as much of the
flavour is in the skin, especially with large mushrooms.
Onions and potatoes should be kept dry and in the dark.
A cardboard box with newspaper on top is fine. Don't eat
potatoes that have gone green.

VERMOUTH, SHERRY AND WINE
There are never any half-drunk bottles of wine in my
kitchen waiting to be added to a recipe so I rely on dry
white vermouth and dry sherry, both relatively inexpensive and a bottle goes a long way. You can also buy dry
red and white wine in handy small cans.

4. ESPECIALLY FOR FISH LOVERS

TUNA FISH STIR FRY

Serves two   *Takes approx. 12 mins.*

This is a very quick combination of tuna and vegetables with a light lemony glaze. I have used canned sweetcorn and beansprouts as I find them handy items to have in the cupboard, but please use the fresh variety if you prefer.

Serve the Tuna Fish Stir Fry in shallow bowls with crusty rolls.

2 tbsp (30ml) soy sauce
1 tbsp (15ml) tomato purée
2 tbsp (30ml) lemon juice
1 tsp (5ml) clear honey
2 tbsp (30ml) cold water
Salt and freshly milled pepper
2 tsp (10ml) cornflour
425g can baby corn on the cob
410g can beansprouts
1 medium onion
3 sticks celery

(continued opposite)

(Tuna Fish Stir Fry continued)

7 oz (198g) can tuna in oil
1 large slice bread
1 tbsp (15ml) oil

1. Measure the soy sauce, tomato purée, lemon juice, honey and water into a small bowl. Add seasoning to taste and whisk together. Sprinkle the cornflour over and whisk until smooth. Set aside.
2. Tip the corn and beansprouts into a sieve and leave to drain.
3. Peel and very thinly slice the onion. Cut the celery into very thin slices. Set aside.
4. Drain the tuna, reserving the oil. Break the tuna into chunks. Place the tuna oil in the frypan.
5. Cut the bread into small cubes.
6. Heat the oil, add the bread cubes and cook over medium-high heat, stirring constantly, until golden brown. Remove and keep hot.
7. Add the 1 tbsp (15ml) oil to the pan and stir in the onion and celery. Cook over medium-high heat, stirring constantly, until soft but not brown.
8. Add the corn and beansprouts and continue to cook, stirring constantly, for a further 3 mins. or until very hot.
9. Remove from the heat and add the tuna.
10. Whisk the soy mixture (in case the cornflour has settled to the bottom of the bowl) and pour over the stir fry.
11. Return to the heat and cook for a further minute or two until the glaze has come to the boil, thickened slightly and coated the vegetables.
12. Spoon into two warm serving bowls and serve immediately, sprinkled with the croûtons.

TROUT FILLETS WITH GRAPES
Serves two　　　　　　　　*Takes approx. 15 mins.*

Impressive – but so simple to cook! Be cautious with the pinch of cayenne unless you like really hot spiced food. For a milder flavour use paprika. Other fish fillets may be used instead of the trout.

Serve with hot rice and very lightly cooked mangetout or whole green beans.

4 oz (100g) white grapes
3 fl oz (75ml) dry white vermouth
2 fl oz (50ml) cold water
Very small pinch cayenne pepper
1 vegetable stock cube
2 large or 4 small trout fillets
1 tbsp (15ml) seasoned flour
1 oz (25g) butter
4 tbsp (60ml) 8% fromage frais or sour cream
Salt and freshly milled pepper

1. Halve the grapes and remove the pips. Set aside. Combine the vermouth, water, pepper and crumbled stock cube.
2. Lightly coat the trout fillets with seasoned flour.
3. Heat the butter in the frypan, slip in the trout skin-side down and cook over medium heat until golden brown, turning over once.
4. Remove the trout to heated plates and keep warm.
5. Carefully pour the seasoned wine/stock into the pan and bring to the boil, stirring. Allow to boil until it has bubbled to half the quantity. Reduce the heat to low.
6. Stir in the fromage frais until smooth and season to taste. Add the grapes and heat for 30 seconds. Spoon over the trout and serve immediately.

SPICED FISH STIR FRY

Serves two   *Takes approx. 10 mins.*

Very lightly spiced fish, with just a hint of warmth in the
sauce rather than a strong curry flavour, and vegetables in
a creamy sauce. Choose boneless skinned cuts of a chunky
firm fish such as cod, haddock, monkfish or salmon. If
available, fresh tuna or swordfish is delicious too.

Just serve with hot bread, perhaps with garlic or herb
butter.

8 oz (225g) young carrots
8 oz (225g) young whole green beans
1 vegetable stock cube
¼ pt (150ml) boiling water
1 tbsp (15ml) flour
½ tsp (2.5ml) ground cumin
½ tsp (2.5ml) ground coriander
½ tsp (2.5ml) mild paprika
12 oz (350g) boneless skinned fish
1 oz (25g) butter
4 tbsp (60ml) double cream
Salt and freshly ground pepper

1. Peel or scrub the carrots and cut into matchsticks.
    Top and tail the beans and slice diagonally into 1 in/
    2.5cm lengths. Set aside. Dissolve the stock cube in
    the water.
2. On a sheet of greaseproof paper, combine the flour
    and spices.
3. Cut the fish into 1 in/2.5cm cubes. Coat on all sides
    with the spiced flour.
4. Heat the butter in the frypan and add the fish. Cook,
    turning gently, over medium-high heat until golden
    brown on all sides. Remove from the pan and keep
    hot.
5. Add the vegetables and stock to the pan. Bring just to
    the boil then reduce the heat. Cover and simmer
    gently until the vegetables are just cooked, about 4
    mins.
6. Stir in the cream and season to taste. Add the fish and
    cook for a further minute to heat the fish through.
    Serve immediately.

CHEESY FISH
Serves two   *Takes approx. 15 mins.*

The combination of fish, cheese and bacon is a favourite with most people, especially the cook if they are all in a very fast one-dish recipe. Any type of white fish fillets or cutlets is suitable for this dish.

Serve with a jacket potato or simply very hot unbuttered granary toast.

3 oz (75g) mature Cheddar cheese
1 tbsp (15ml) cornflour
Salt and freshly milled pepper
½ tsp (2.5ml) nutmeg
½ pt (300ml) milk
1 small onion
4 oz (100g) young carrots
2 oz (50g) streaky bacon
8 oz (225g) white fish fillets or cutlets

1. Grate the cheese. Whisk the cornflour, salt, pepper and nutmeg into the milk. Set aside.
2. Peel and finely chop the onion. Peel or scrub the carrots and cut into very thin slices.
3. Cut the bacon into thin strips. Tip into the frypan and cook, stirring, over medium-high heat until the bacon begins to brown.
4. Add the onion and carrot, stirring to coat with the bacon fat. Continue to cook, stirring, until they are soft but not brown. Remove from the heat.
5. Whisk the seasoned milk again (the cornflour may have sunk to the bottom) and add to the pan.
6. Reduce the heat to low and cook, stirring constantly, until the sauce just comes to the boil and is thickened. Add 2 oz (50g) of the cheese, stirring until melted.
7. Add the fish to the pan, spooning over the sauce to cover it. Cook over low heat for 5–6 mins. or until the fish is opaque and flakes easily.
8. Serve immediately on warm plates, sprinkling with the remaining cheese.

FISH AND FENNEL SAUTÉ

Serves two *Takes approx. 25 mins.*

A delicious combination of white fish, potatoes and fennel in a cream and wine sauce. Use a firm fish such as cod, haddock or halibut. If you are using frozen fish allow extra cooking time in step 5. Fennel is a white bulbous vegetable similar in appearance and texture to celery but has an aniseed flavour. Choose white or pale-green firm bulbs with fresh, feathery leaves. When fennel is out of season, use a small head of celery.

I like to serve Cheese and Tomato Bread with this dish. Simply blend equal quantities of butter and grated Cheddar cheese together, then add a dash of tomato purée. Cut a Vienna or French loaf as for garlic bread and spread the flavoured butter on the cut surfaces. Place on a baking sheet and heat through in a hot oven.

8 oz (225g) potatoes
4 oz (100g) young carrots
1 small fennel bulb
1 clove garlic
4 spring onions
1 vegetable stock cube
8 fl oz (225ml) boiling water
2 fl oz (50ml) dry white vermouth
2 tsp (10ml) freeze-dried Fines Herbes
12 oz (350g) firm white fish
½ oz (15g) butter
5 tbsp (75ml) double cream
Salt and freshly milled pepper

1. Peel the potatoes and cut into ½ in/1cm cubes. Trim, peel or scrub the carrots. Cut into similar-sized cubes and add to the potato. Trim the root and stem ends of the fennel, reserving any feathery leaves as a garnish. Cut in half lengthwise then each half into six wedges. Peel and crush the garlic. Trim the spring onions. Thinly slice the green tops and set aside as a garnish. Cut the white parts into ½ in/1cm pieces.
2. Dissolve the stock cube in the boiling water and add

the vermouth and Fines Herbes. Cut the fish into 1 in/ 2cm cubes.

3. Heat the butter in the frypan and add the potatoes and carrots. Cook over medium-high heat, stirring constantly, until the potatoes begin to brown, about 4 mins.

4. Add the fennel wedges, garlic, white parts of the spring onions and the stock/wine. Cover and reduce the heat to a gentle simmer. Cook until the vegetables are just tender, about 10 mins.

5. Add the cubes of fish and continue to cook, covered, until they are just firm and opaque, about 5 mins.

6. Stir in the cream and heat through for 1 min. Season to taste. Spoon into warm shallow bowls and sprinkle with the green spring onion pieces. Garnish with fennel leaves and serve immediately.

CRISP-COATED SALMON IN MUSHROOM AND PERNOD SAUCE

Serves two   *Takes approx. 15 mins.*

Salmon is a dry fish but coating the portions with crumbs keeps it moist and succulent. Other boneless fish steaks or fillets would be just as good. No Pernod? Use dry white vermouth or whisky.

This richly flavoured dish needs only to be served with freshly cooked pasta such as tagliatelle and a salad of thinly sliced cucumber sprinkled with salt and pepper plus a dash of white wine vinegar.

1 egg
5 fl oz (150ml) double cream
2 tbsp (30ml) Pernod
2 salmon steaks or fillets
1 tbsp (15ml) seasoned flour
1 oz (25g) fresh breadcrumbs
1 oz (25g) butter
4 oz (100g) button mushrooms
1 vegetable stock cube
5 fl oz (150ml) cold water
Salt and freshly milled pepper

1. Separate the egg, tipping the yolk into a small bowl and the white onto a plate.
2. Add the cream and Pernod to the yolk and lightly beat together to blend in the yolk. Set aside.
3. Lightly whisk the white with a fork.
4. Coat the salmon first with seasoned flour, then with the egg white and finally with the breadcrumbs, pressing them on with your fingers.
5. Heat half the butter in the frypan, slide in the fish and cook over medium heat, turning over once, until the fish tests cooked. (Gently open up the centre with two forks, the fish should be opaque and firm when fully cooked.)
6. Remove from the pan onto heated plates and keep warm.
7. Heat the remaining butter, toss in the mushrooms and cook, stirring, until golden. Crumble the stock cube into the water, add to the pan and bring to the boil. Allow to boil until reduced to half the quantity. Remove from the heat.
8. Blend in the cream mixture and continue to cook over low heat until the sauce slightly thickens. Do not allow it to boil. Season to taste.
9. Pour over the salmon and serve immediately.

PLAICE AND CRAB ROLLS WITH MUSHROOM SAUCE
Serves two   *Takes approx. 15 mins.*

Look for dressed crab among the selection of canned and bottled sandwich fillings. It has a rich flavour which combines well with the plaice and the creamy wine-flavoured sauce. Choose either the 1% or 8% fat content fromage frais. Both add smoothness to the sauce with minimal calories.

I like to serve the Plaice and Crab Rolls with freshly cooked rice or mashed potatoes and lightly cooked whole green beans.

1 large slice fresh bread
1 lemon
43g can dressed crab
1 tbsp (15ml) chopped parsley
Freshly milled pepper
4 small skinned plaice fillets
4 rashers streaky bacon
1 vegetable stock cube
5 fl oz (150ml) boiling water
2 fl oz (50ml) dry white vermouth
1 oz (25g) soft butter
2 tsp (10ml) flour
4 oz (100g) button mushrooms
3 tbsp (45ml) fromage frais

1. Cut off the bread crust and make into crumbs (with a food processor or grater). Tip into a medium bowl.
2. Cut the lemon in half and squeeze the juice from one half. Thinly slice the other half and reserve for the garnish. Add the lemon juice, crab and parsley to the crumbs. Season with pepper and mix thoroughly together.
3. Place the fish skinned-side uppermost on the work surface. Divide the crab mixture into four portions and spread each over the fish. Roll up from the tail end.
4. Remove any rind from the bacon and wrap each fish roll in a rasher, securing the ends with wooden cocktail sticks. Set aside.
5. Dissolve the stock cube in the water and add the vermouth. Using half of the butter, blend in the flour to make a smooth mixture. Slice the mushrooms. Set stock, butter mixture and mushrooms aside.
6. Melt the remaining butter in the frypan and add the fish rolls. Cook over medium heat, turning frequently, until golden brown on all sides. Remove from the pan.
7. Add the mushrooms to the pan and cook for 2 mins. until beginning to brown. Off the heat, stir in the stock. Return to the heat and bring just to the boil.
8. Return the fish to the pan, cover and simmer gently over low heat for 10 mins. Lift out the fish onto warm

plates and keep warm.

9. Bring the stock and mushrooms back to the boil. Add the butter and flour mixture gradually to the pan, stirring constantly until thickened and smooth. Stir in the fromage frais and cook for 30 seconds longer.

10. Spoon over the fish and serve immediately, garnished with the reserved lemon slices.

MANDARIN PRAWNS
Serves two   *Takes approx. 12 mins.*

A special treat for shellfish lovers, no-one will believe how simple the recipe is – so why tell them! If using frozen prawns, thaw and dry them well. Just a few mangetout or sugarsnap peas add a very special touch to a stir fry dish. Just snip off the 'tops and tails' with a sharp knife, rinse and dry on paper towel.

The portions of Mandarin Prawns, with the colourful vegetables, are very generous. If wished, serve with a simple green salad. For dessert, combine well chilled melon balls, lychees and sliced kiwi fruit and serve with fortune cookies.

6 oz (175g) Chinese egg noodles
2 tsp (10ml) cornflour
1 tbsp (15ml) cold water
3 tbsp (45ml) soy sauce
3 tbsp (45ml) dry sherry
3 tbsp (45ml) tomato ketchup
1 red pepper
4 oz (100g) mangetout OR sugarsnap peas
6 spring onions
2 cloves garlic
1 oz (25g) butter
8 oz (225g) cooked and shelled large prawns, thawed if frozen
Salt and freshly milled pepper

1. Cook the Chinese noodles according to package directions.

2. In a small bowl, blend the cornflour and water together until smooth. Stir in the soy sauce, sherry and ketchup. Set aside.
3. Cut the pepper into thin rings, discarding the stem, pith and seeds. Trim the mangetout (or sugarsnap peas) and spring onions, cutting the onions diagonally into 2 in/5cm pieces. Add the mangetout and onions to the pepper.
4. Peel and crush the garlic. Heat the butter in the frypan and stir in the garlic and vegetables. Cook, stirring constantly, over medium-high heat for 2–3 mins. or until just beginning to soften.
5. Stir in the prawns and continue to cook, stirring, for about 3 mins.
6. Stir the cornflour mixture and pour over the vegetables and prawns. Cook, stirring, just until the glaze thickens and coats the stir fry – about 1 min.
7. Drain the noodles. Add to the frypan and very lightly toss with the vegetables and prawns. Serve immediately.

FISH ANDALOUSE
Serves two   *Takes approx. 12 mins.*

Choose any firm white fish, either cutlets or fillets, to cook in this rich tomato and anchovy sauce.

Complete the meal with hot garlic bread, a simple green salad, and chilled grapes for dessert.

1 medium onion
1 clove garlic
50g can anchovy fillets
1 tbsp (15ml) flour
Salt and freshly milled pepper
2 fish cutlets or fillets
1 tbsp (15ml) olive oil
2 tbsp (30ml) red wine vinegar
8.1 oz (230g) can chopped tomatoes

(continued opposite)

(Fish Andalouse continued)

2 tsp (10ml) sugar
2 tsp (10ml) fresh or freeze-dried thyme
1 oz (25g) pitted green olives

1. Peel and thinly slice the onion. Peel and crush the garlic and add to the onion. Drain the anchovies and chop half of them, reserving the remainder for garnish. Set aside.
2. Tip the flour onto a sheet of greaseproof paper and season lightly. Coat the fish with the seasoned flour, pressing on with your fingertips.
3. Heat the oil in the frypan and slide in the fish. Cook over medium-high heat until golden brown on both sides. Remove from the pan with a slotted spoon and set aside.
4. Add the onion and garlic to the pan and cook, stirring, until soft and golden brown – about 2 mins. Stir in the chopped anchovies, vinegar, tomatoes, sugar and thyme. Bring to the boil.
5. Reduce the heat to a medium-low and return the fish to the pan. Cover and simmer gently, carefully turning the fish once, until the fish is cooked through. The time will vary depending on the cut and thickness of the fish. When fully cooked, it should flake easily and be opaque throughout.
6. Add the olives, sliced if wished, and serve immediately, garnished with the reserved whole anchovies.

MANHATTAN SEAFOOD STEW
Serves two   *Takes approx. 20 mins.*

This is my version of the Manhattan seafood chowder, a richly flavoured fish soup packed with clams and tomatoes. If you can find some clams, use them instead of the prawns.

Serve the Seafood Stew piping hot in bowls with spoons and forks and lots of garlic bread. Follow it New York style with wedges of creamy cheesecake from the supermarket.

1 medium onion
8 oz (225g) potatoes
12 oz (350g) cod fillets
2 tbsp (30ml) flour
1 tsp (5ml) paprika
Salt and freshly milled pepper
2 tbsp (30ml) olive oil
1 vegetable stock cube
5 fl oz (150ml) boiling water
8.1 oz (230g) can chopped tomatoes
2 tsp (10ml) granulated sugar
2 tsp (10ml) fresh thyme OR 1 tsp (5ml) freeze-dried
4 oz (100g) cooked prawns
2 lemon wedges

1. Peel the onion and chop finely. Peel the potatoes and cut into ½ in/1cm dice. Add to the onion and set aside.
2. Remove the skin from the fish (your fishmonger will do this for you) and cut into large cubes (about 2 in/5cm). Check for and remove any stray bones.
3. On a sheet of greaseproof paper, blend together the flour, paprika, salt and pepper. Add the fish and toss together to coat it evenly with the seasoned flour.
4. Heat half the oil in the frypan, add the fish and cook over medium heat until golden brown on all sides, turning frequently. Remove from the pan.
5. Add the remaining oil to the pan, toss in the potatoes and onion. Increase the heat to high and cook, stirring constantly, until golden brown. Crumble the stock

cube over, add the boiling water, the tomatoes, sugar and the thyme. Stir well, cover, reduce to a gentle simmer and cook until the potatoes are tender, about 10 mins.

6. Return the fish to the pan with the prawns. Cook a few minutes longer to heat them through. Serve immediately garnished with the lemon wedges.

TROUT KEDGEREE
Serves two   *Takes approx. 10 mins.*

First served as a breakfast dish in the eighteenth century, kedgeree is traditionally made with smoked fish. Now that we are more likely to eat breakfast on the run, enjoy this lighter version made with trout fillets at lunch or supper. The spice quantities are light – if you prefer a stronger curry flavour be more generous. Use cooked rice left over from a previous meal (4 oz (100g) uncooked weight) or a 277g can of ready-cooked long grain rice.

I like to serve the Trout Kedgeree with a salad of crisp lettuce and sliced, raw, button mushrooms, tossed with a herby oil and vinegar dressing.

1 tsp (5ml) paprika
1 tsp (5ml) turmeric
1 tsp (5ml) ground cumin
1 tsp (5ml) ground coriander
¼ tsp (1.25ml) chilli powder
12 oz (350g) skinned trout fillets
1 large onion
1 oz (25g) butter
8 oz (225g) cooked rice (see above)
5 fl oz (150ml) single cream
Salt and freshly milled pepper

1. Measure the spices into a small bowl and mix together. Slice the trout fillets across into 1 in/2.5cm strips. Set aside.
2. Peel and thinly slice the onion. Melt the butter in the

frypan and stir in the onion. Cook, stirring, over medium-high heat until golden brown – 2–3 mins.

3. Sprinkle the spices over and stir well. Continue to cook, stirring, for 1–2 mins; cooking the spices brings out their flavours.

4. Add the trout and continue to cook, stirring very gently to avoid breaking up the fish, until it is lightly browned.

5. Reduce the heat to medium and sprinkle the rice over (if using left-over rice, separate the grains with your fingertips first. Pour the cream over and lightly stir to combine.

6. Continue to heat until bubbling hot. Season to taste then serve immediately.

5. POPULAR POULTRY

CHEESY CHICKEN WITH RICE
Serves two   *Takes approx. 20 mins.*

Tender chicken breasts stuffed with herbs and cheese, complete with rice and vegetables. Instead of the can of cooked rice – a very useful store cupboard stand-by – use 4–6 oz (100–175g) cooked rice left over from a previous meal.

While the chicken is simmering make a simple salad of cherry tomatoes, diced cucumber and sliced spring onions, tossed with a little oil and vinegar dressing.

1 clove garlic
1 tbsp (15ml) chopped parsley
1 tbsp (15ml) chopped chives
2 oz (50g) curd cheese
2 large skinned and boned chicken breasts
2 rashers smoked streaky bacon
1 chicken stock cube
⅓ pt (220ml) boiling water
2 fl oz (50ml) dry sherry
½ oz (15g) butter
277g can ready cooked rice

(continued overleaf)

(Cheesy Chicken With Rice continued)

2 oz (50g) frozen peas
2 oz (50g) canned or frozen sweetcorn kernels
Salt and freshly milled pepper
Sprigs of parsley or chives for garnish

1. Peel and crush the garlic onto a plate. Add the chopped herbs and the curd cheese. With a flexible knife thoroughly blend them together. Divide into two portions.
2. Place the chicken breasts on the work surface rounded side uppermost. Holding a small sharp knife horizontally, cut a slit two-thirds of the way into the chicken to form a 'pocket'.
3. Place a portion of herbed cheese inside each pocket. Trim any rinds from the bacon and wrap a rasher around each chicken breast, securing the ends with wooden cocktail sticks. Set aside.
4. Dissolve the stock cube in the water and add the sherry. Set aside.
5. Melt the butter in the frypan and add the chicken. Cook over medium-high heat, turning frequently, until golden brown on all sides.
6. Off the heat, to avoid splattering, add the stock. Reduce the heat to medium-low. Cover and gently simmer until the chicken is tender, turning the chicken once – about 10 mins. Remove the chicken from the pan and keep hot.
7. Stir the rice, peas and corn into the pan juices. Increase the heat to medium-high and cook, stirring, until they are very hot. Season to taste.
8. Remove the cocktail sticks and cut the chicken diagonally into thick slices. Arrange them on warm plates and add the rice. Garnish with the herbs and serve immediately.

HERB AND LEMON CHICKEN
Serves two　　　　　　　　　　　*Takes approx. 20 mins.*

Chicken thighs are a good budget buy with a high proportion of meat to bone and a good flavour, but they do need slower cooking than white chicken meat. Fresh herbs always add the best flavour to a dish but when not available choose freeze-dried herbs. These have a good colour and an almost fresh flavour. Buy in small jars, keep away from the light and use quickly.

Serve the chicken with hot garlic bread and chilled potato salad from the supermarket.

1 lemon
3 tbsp (45ml) chopped fresh parsley
1 medium onion
1 yellow or red pepper
1 tbsp (15ml) olive oil
4 large chicken thighs
8.1 oz (230g) can chopped tomatoes
2 tbsp (30ml) chopped fresh mixed herbs OR
**　1 tbsp (15ml) freeze-dried**
Salt and freshly milled black pepper
8 black olives (optional)

1. Finely grate the lemon rind and mix into the chopped parsley. Set aside. Squeeze the lemon and set the juice aside.
2. Peel the onion and thinly slice. Cut the pepper into thin rings, discarding the stem, seeds and any pith.
3. Heat the oil in the frypan, add the onion and pepper and cook over medium heat, stirring, until soft.
4. Push the vegetables to one side of the pan and add the chicken thighs (skinned if wished). Increase the heat and cook, turning the chicken until golden brown on all sides.
5. Add the tomatoes, lemon juice and mixed herbs. Reduce the heat to a gentle simmer, cover and cook for 15 mins. or until the chicken is tender and cooked through. Season to taste and add the olives.
6. Serve sprinkled with the lemon and parsley mixture.

STILTON-STUFFED CHICKEN IN ORANGE SAUCE

Serves two   *Takes approx. 25 mins.*

Chicken thighs are easy to bone and are very meaty. Here, stuffed with Stilton cheese and wrapped in bacon, they are then gently simmered in a sweet-sharp sauce.

Serve the Stilton-Stuffed Chicken with fluffy mashed potatoes or rice, or simply with crusty bread and a mixed green salad. Garnish with additional fresh orange segments if wished.

4 large chicken thighs
2 oz (50g) Stilton cheese
4 rashers back bacon
1 large orange
1 tbsp (25g) cornflour
3 tbsp (45ml) dry white vermouth
2 tbsp (30ml) marmalade
1 oz (25g) butter
Salt and freshly milled pepper

1. Remove the chicken skin. Using a small sharp knife cut through the flesh along the length of the bone. Open out and continue to cut as close to the bone as possible until you can lift the bone out. Discard the bones.
2. Cut the cheese into four fingers and insert one into each piece of chicken. Remove any bacon rinds and wrap a rasher around each chicken piece, securing with a wooden toothpick.
3. Finely grate the orange rind and squeeze the orange for juice. Place rind and juice in a small bowl and sprinkle the cornflour over. Add the vermouth and whisk until smooth. Stir in the marmalade. Set aside.
4. Heat the butter in the frypan. Add the chicken pieces and cook over medium-high heat, turning frequently, until golden brown on all sides. Remove from the pan.
5. Whisk the cornflour liquid then stir into the pan, scraping up the sediment on the base. Bring just to the boil, stirring until smooth. Season to taste.
6. Return the chicken to the pan. Cover and reduce the heat to a gentle simmer. Cook for 20 mins. Serve immediately.

CHICKEN WITH MUSTARD CREAM SAUCE
Serves two   *Takes approx. 12 mins.*

Delicious to eat, this recipe is much simpler to prepare than it looks. I have used skinned chicken breasts but equally good is any turkey portion such as fillets. Other chicken-portions such as quarters or thighs could be used but allow extra cooking time in step 3.

There is plenty of the sauce, so serve with rice or mashed potatoes and a mixed salad.

1 oz (25g) butter
2 tsp (10ml) flour
1 vegetable stock cube
⅓ pt (200ml) boiling water
2 boned and skinned chicken breasts
1 tbsp (15ml) whole-grain mustard
4 tbsp (60ml) double cream
Salt and freshly milled pepper

1. Using a flat plate and a flexible knife, cream together half the butter and the flour until quite soft and smooth. Set aside. Dissolve the stock cube in the water.
2. Heat the remaining butter in the frypan, add the chicken skinned-side uppermost. Cook over medium-high heat turning frequently, until golden brown on all sides.
3. Add the stock to the pan, cover and reduce the heat to medium. Simmer for about 8 mins, or until the chicken is cooked through. (To check that boneless chicken breasts are cooked, press with the finger. The flesh will spring back when cooked through. Pierce bone-in portions with a fork. The juices will run clear when fully cooked.) Remove the chicken and keep hot.
4. Gradually add the creamed butter and flour mixture (this is called a 'beurre manie') in flakes to the stock, stirring constantly. (Remember not to use a wire whisk if cooking in a non-stick frypan.) Allow the sauce to simmer gently but do not boil.
5. Stir in the mustard and cream. Add salt and pepper if wished. Return the chicken to the pan and gently heat for a minute or two. Serve immediately.

CHICKEN, FENNEL AND ORANGE STIR FRY

Serves two   *Takes approx. 12 mins.*

A speedy and very fresh-tasting stir fry of chicken, sweet pepper and fennel with the unexpected addition of fresh oranges. Fennel has a mild aniseed flavour – if preferred, use the tender inside sticks of celery instead.

Serve with Chinese noodles if wished, or simply with warm rolls and a green salad.

2 oranges
Boiling water
2 tsp (10ml) cornflour
2 tbsp (30ml) soy sauce
1 medium bulb of fennel
1 small red pepper
1 small yellow pepper
6 spring onions
2 skinned and boned chicken breasts
1 tbsp (15ml) olive oil
Salt and freshly milled pepper

1. Using a swivel potato peeler cut off just the orange part of the peel of one orange (this is called the zest). Cut into needle-sized shreds and cover with boiling water. Set aside. Carefully remove the remaining white pith from this orange. With a small, sharp knife, cut between the membranes to remove each orange segment, allowing it to drop onto a plate. Remove any seeds and set aside.
2. Squeeze the juice from the second orange into a small bowl. Whisk in the cornflour and soy sauce. Set aside.
3. Trim the base and top of the fennel and cut into quarters. Cut each quarter into four thin wedges.
4. Halve both the red and yellow peppers, discarding the stem, pith and seeds. Cut into thin slices. Trim the spring onions and finely shred the green tops, reserving them for the garnish. Cut the white parts into diagonal ½ in/1cm slices.
5. Cut the chicken breasts into thin fingers.
6. Heat the oil in the frypan, add the chicken and cook

over medium-high heat until beginning to brown, stirring constantly.

7. Add the vegetables, including the white parts of the spring onions, and continue to cook, stirring constantly, until the vegetables are just soft (they should still be slightly crisp).
8. Pour the orange juice/cornflour over and cook, stirring constantly, until the chicken and vegetables are coated with the glaze. Season to taste.
9. Very gently add the orange segments and heat for 30 seconds.
10. Drain the orange zest.
11. Spoon the stir fry on to warm plates. Sprinkle the orange zest and the chopped spring onion tops over it. Serve immediately.

CHICKEN SALAD JEREZ
Serves two   *Takes approx. 7 mins.*

The combination of hot and cold ingredients when least expected adds fun to eating! You would expect a stir fry combination of bacon, chicken and chicken livers to be served with noodles but I have piled it atop crisp salad greens, added the hot sherry-based dressing and lightly tossed it all together. Choose a selection of very crisp salad greens such as Chinese leaves or cos lettuce, chicory or tiny Tom Thumb lettuces that will not go limp with the hot dressing.

Serve immediately with hot crisp breads.

Enough crisp salad greens for two portions (see above)
1 small sweet red onion
1 tbsp (15ml) olive oil
2 tbsp (30ml) dry sherry
2 tsp (10ml) coarse grain mustard
2 tsp (10ml) sugar
4 rashers smoked streaky bacon
1 large skinned and boned chicken breast

(continued overleaf)

(Chicken Salad Jerez continued)

4 oz (100g) chicken livers (thawed if bought frozen)
1 clove garlic
Salt and freshly milled pepper

1. Wash the salad greens and very thoroughly dry in a tea-towel (wet salad greens ruin a salad). Tear into bite-sized pieces with your fingers and place in a large salad bowl. Peel and very thinly slice the onion. Separate the slices into rings and add to the bowl. Set aside.
2. Whisk together the oil, sherry, mustard and sugar. Set aside.
3. Remove any rind from the bacon and cut across into ½ in/1cm strips. Cut the chicken breast into ½ in/1cm slices. Cut the chicken livers into bite-sized pieces. Peel and crush the garlic.
4. Cook the bacon and garlic in the frypan over medium heat, stirring constantly, until the bacon is crisp. Add the chicken and increase the heat to medium-high. Continue to cook, stirring constantly, until golden brown. Stir in the chicken livers and cook, stirring, until they have lost their pinkness.
5. Season with salt and pepper and add to the salad bowl.
6. Pour the oil mixture into the pan and allow to bubble for a few seconds, stirring to scrape off any sediment on the bottom of the pan.
7. Pour over the salad and toss lightly but thoroughly. Serve IMMEDIATELY!

CHICKEN VENEZIA
Serves two   *Takes approx. 25 mins.*

In Italian markets basil is sold in enormous pungent, peppery bouquets while here we have to be content with tiny buttonhole-sized sprigs. To compensate, Italy exports this delicious herb to us as pesto – a combination of finely chopped basil, pinenuts, Parmesan cheese and olive oil. Just a spoonful adds a special taste to sauces and salad dressings. In this recipe it flavours the stuffing spooned under the skin of chicken breasts. Once opened, remember to smooth the top of the remaining pesto in the jar and cover with a thin layer of olive oil to prevent it spoiling. Store in the fridge.

Serve Chicken Venezia with Italian Ciabetta bread.

1 large slice fresh bread
1 tbsp (15ml) pesto sauce
4 tbsp (60ml) curd cheese
2 large boned chicken breasts
1 small lemon
1 chicken stock cube
4 fl oz (100ml) boiling water
3 fl oz (75ml) dry white vermouth
8 oz (225g) small courgettes
1 small onion
1 tbsp (15ml) olive oil
Salt and freshly milled pepper

1. Trim the crust from the bread and make into crumbs with a grater or food processor.
2. In a small bowl beat the pesto into the cheese. Gradually blend in the crumbs.
3. Carefully loosen the skin of the chicken from the flesh to form a pocket. Spread half of the pesto stuffing into each pocket. Smooth the skin over the stuffing and set the chicken breasts aside.
4. Cut half the lemon into thin slices. Cut the remaining half into two wedges for the garnish. Set aside.
5. Dissolve the stock cube in the water and add the vermouth.
6. Trim the ends of the courgettes and cut into 1 in/

2.5cm slices. Peel and thinly slice the onion.

7. Heat the oil in the frypan and add the chicken breasts. Cook over medium-high heat until golden brown on all sides, turning carefully with two spoons. (Don't worry if some of the stuffing falls out, it will blend with the vegetables.) Remove from the pan.

8. Add the onion to the pan and cook over medium-high heat, stirring constantly, for 1–2 mins. to soften. Add the courgettes and continue to cook, stirring, until they are pale golden brown.

9. Add the lemon slices and the stock/vermouth. Bring just to the boil then reduce the heat to medium-low.

10. Return the chicken breasts to the pan skin-side uppermost. Cover and simmer gently until the chicken is tender and cooked, 15–20 mins.

11. Serve the chicken and vegetables on warm plates, garnished with the lemon wedges. Serve immediately.

CREAMED CHICKEN AND MUSHROOMS
Serves two   *Takes approx. 10 mins.*

Chicken and mushrooms gently simmered in a sherry sauce. Don't skip the lemon and parsley – it looks very pretty and tastes good too.

Serve the Fricassee with rice or a jacket potato – or, as I prefer for a very quick meal, spooned over thick slices of hot granary toast.

1 medium lemon
1 tbsp (15ml) chopped fresh parsley
4 oz (100g) button mushrooms
4 large skinned and boned chicken thighs
2 tsp (10ml) flour
Salt and freshly milled pepper
½ tsp (2.5ml) paprika
1 medium onion
1 oz (25g) butter
7 fl oz (200ml) milk
2 tbsp (30ml) dry sherry

1. Finely grate the lemon rind and squeeze the lemon for juice. Add the rind to the parsley. Slice the mushrooms. Set aside.
2. Cut each chicken thigh into thin strips. On a sheet of greaseproof paper combine the flour, salt, pepper and paprika. Add the chicken and toss to coat with the flour. Set aside.
3. Peel and thinly slice the onion. Heat the butter in the frypan and stir in the onion. Cook, stirring, over medium-high heat until soft. Add the mushrooms and continue to cook, stirring, until both vegetables are beginning to brown.
4. Add the chicken, including any unused seasoned flour. Continue to cook, stirring, for 4–5 mins. or until chicken is cooked. Remove from the heat.
5. Gradually stir in the milk and sherry. Return to the heat and cook, stirring, until the sauce comes to the boil and is smooth and thickened. Season to taste with the lemon juice.
6. Spoon onto the hot toast and sprinkle with the lemon and parsley. Serve immediately.

NORMANDY CHICKEN
Serves two   *Takes approx. 15 mins.*

Definitely a dish to impress; tender chicken in a rich apple-flavoured cream sauce – add a dash of Calvados (or brandy) with the stock, if you have a bottle to hand.

Serve with freshly cooked rice or pasta, or simply just a sharp-flavoured salad such as pink grapefruit segments piled onto baby lettuce leaves. Lightly sprinkle with oil and vinegar dressing and freshly milled black pepper.

2 large boneless chicken breasts
1 small onion
2 sticks celery
1 small eating apple
1 vegetable or chicken stock cube

(continued overleaf)

(Normandy Chicken continued)

¼ pt (150ml) boiling water
1 oz (25g) butter
½ oz (15g) flaked almonds
2 tsp (10ml) plain flour
A pinch of ground cloves
Salt and freshly ground pepper
5 fl oz (150ml) dry cider
2 fl oz (50ml) double cream

1. If wished, skin the chicken breasts. Peel and very thinly slice the onion. Thinly slice the celery, reserving any leaves. Add celery to the onion and set aside. Cut the apple into four wedges and remove the core. Dissolve the stock cube in the water.
2. Melt half the butter in the frypan, stir in the almonds and gently cook until golden brown, stirring constantly. Remove with a slotted spoon onto paper towel. Set aside.
3. Add the apple wedges to the pan and cook gently until lightly brown. Remove and set aside.
4. Melt remaining butter in the frypan, add the chicken, skin (or skinned) -side uppermost, and cook over medium heat, turning frequently, until golden. Remove with a slotted spoon.
5. Add the onion and celery to the pan and cook, stirring, until they begin to soften, about 2 mins. Sprinkle over the flour, cloves and seasoning. Stir in the cider and stock, and bring to the boil, stirring until smooth.
6. Return the chicken to the pan, skin (or skinned) -side uppermost. Gently simmer for 5 mins. or until chicken is cooked through. Stir in the cream and check seasoning.
7. Serve sprinkled with the buttered almonds and garnished with the apple slices and reserved celery leaves.

FRUITED CHICKEN CURRY
Serves two   *Takes approx. 25 mins.*

The dark meat of chicken thighs has more flavour but does need slower cooking than the breast meat. Jars of curry paste come in mild or hotter versions. Choose the one to suit your taste and store the opened jar in the refrigerator.

Serve the curry with rice or warm naan breads.

1 tbsp (15ml) mint jelly
3 fl oz (75ml) natural yoghurt
1 small eating apple
1 small banana
2 tsp (10ml) lemon juice
1 medium onion
2 garlic cloves
4 large chicken thighs
½ oz (15g) butter
1 tsp (5ml) oil
1 tsp (5ml) granulated sugar
½ chicken stock cube
1 tbsp (15ml) curry paste
5 fl oz (150ml) boiling water
Salt and freshly ground pepper
Coriander to garnish (optional)

1. Whisk the mint jelly into the yoghurt and set aside.
2. Quarter the apple and remove the core. Peel the banana. Cut apple and banana into thick slices. Toss with the lemon juice.
3. Peel and finely chop the onion. Peel and crush the garlic.
4. Remove the chicken skin, cut each thigh in half lengthwise and remove the bone. (Some supermarkets sell chicken thighs already skinned and boned.)
5. Melt the butter in the frypan, add the oil. Add the chicken pieces and, over high heat, cook, turning frequently, until golden brown. Remove the chicken with a slotted spoon and set aside.
6. Add the onions and garlic to the pan and sprinkle the sugar over. Cook gently, stirring once or twice, until

soft and pale gold.

7. Dissolve the half stock cube and the curry paste in the water. Stir into the pan and add salt and pepper to taste. Bring to the boil. Return the chicken to the pan with the apple and banana slices.

8. Cover and simmer gently until the chicken is cooked through, about 15 mins.

9. Whisk the mint jelly and yoghurt again and serve with the curry, garnished with a coriander sprig, if wished.

GINGER CHICKEN
Serves two   *Takes approx. 15 mins.*

Tender strips of chicken and vegetables in a rich ginger glaze. Hoi-sin (spare-rib) sauce can be found in the oriental food section of most supermarkets. It is made with soy sauce, chilli and sesame seed oil and once opened, should be stored in the fridge. At a pinch, a bottled barbecue sauce could be used instead. For a milder flavour use tomato sauce.

Serve the Ginger Chicken Chinese-style in bowls accompanied by a salad of beansprouts and finely shredded Chinese leaves tossed with oil and vinegar dressing and sprinkled with toasted sunflower seeds.

1 in (2.5cm) fresh ginger root
1 clove garlic
Pinch cayenne pepper
3 tbsp (45ml) hoi-sin sauce
2 tbsp (30ml) soy sauce
1 tbsp (15ml) dry sherry
1 medium onion
1 large green pepper
2 tbsp (30ml) oil
2 oz (50g) cashew nuts
2 large boned and skinned chicken breasts
2 tsp (10ml) cornflour
Salt and freshly milled pepper

1. Peel and finely grate the ginger. Peel the garlic and crush. Add the ginger, garlic and cayenne to the hoi-sin and soy sauce and the sherry. Mix well and set aside.
2. Peel and very thinly slice the onion. Slice the pepper into thin rings, discarding the stem, pith and seeds. Add to the onion and set aside.
3. Heat about 1 tsp (5ml) of the oil in the frypan. Toss in the cashews and cook, stirring constantly, over high heat until golden brown. Tip onto paper towel.
4. Slice the chicken breasts into ½ in/1cm strips. Season the cornflour, add to the chicken and, using your fingers, coat the chicken on all sides.
5. Heat half of the remaining oil, add the chicken and cook, stirring constantly, over high heat until golden brown. Using a slotted spoon, remove to a plate.
6. Add remaining oil to the pan, stir in the onion and pepper and cook, stirring, over medium-high heat until soft and beginning to brown.
7. Stir the hoi-sin sauce mixture, add to the pan and heat to just bubbling. Stir well, add the chicken and cashew nuts and cook, stirring, for 1–2 mins. or until the chicken is piping hot. Serve immediately.

PAPRIKA TURKEY
Serves two   *Takes approx. 25 mins.*

You will find turkey fillets either fresh or frozen. They are inexpensive and, having no skin or bones, are very good value. Look for bottles of concentrated apple juice in healthfood stores. Just a spoonful or two adds a very distinctive apple flavour to a savoury or sweet dish. Remember to store opened bottles in the fridge.

Serve Paprika Turkey with a simple salad of thinly sliced cucumber and chopped spring onions, sprinkled with salt and pepper.

1 medium onion
3 sticks celery

(continued overleaf)

(Paprika Turkey continued)

1 vegetable stock cube
¼ pt (150ml) boiling water
2 tbsp (30ml) concentrated apple juice
1 tbsp (15ml) cider vinegar
1 tbsp (15ml) flour
1 tsp (5ml) paprika
½ tsp (2.5ml) ground mild chilli powder
Salt and freshly milled pepper
4 tbsp (60ml) natural yoghurt
2 large turkey fillets (thawed if frozen)
1 tbsp (15ml) oil
1 tsp (5ml) granulated sugar
8.1oz (230g) can cannellini or butter beans

1. Peel and finely chop the onion. Thinly slice the celery, reserving any leaves for a garnish. Add the slices to the onion and set aside.
2. Crumble the vegetable cube into the water, stir in the apple juice and vinegar. Set aside.
3. On a sheet of greaseproof paper, combine the flour, paprika, chilli powder, salt and pepper. Stir 1 tsp (5ml) into the yoghurt and set aside. Cutting across the turkey fillets, slice them into ½ in/1cm fingers. (If there is a line of membrane up the centre of the fillets, remove this as it may be chewy to eat.) Add the turkey to the seasoned flour and toss to coat completely.
4. Heat half the oil in the frypan, add the turkey (reserve remaining seasoned flour) and cook, stirring constantly, over high heat until golden brown. Using a slotted spoon, remove to a plate.
5. Add the remaining oil to the pan, stir in the onion and celery. Sprinkle with the sugar and any remaining flour. Cook, stirring, over medium heat until soft and pale golden brown.
6. Stir in the stock mixture and return the turkey to the pan. Drain the beans and add to the pan.
7. Cover, reduce the heat and simmer gently for 10–15 mins. or until the turkey is cooked.
8. Stir the thickened yoghurt into the pan and heat through, about 2 mins.
9. Serve immediately, garnished with celery leaves.

TURKEY EN CROÛTE

Serves two   *Takes approx. 20 mins.*

Turkey no longer only appears on sale complete with crisp skin and two plump drumsticks just asking to be eaten with the fingers; turkey escallops are just one of the cuts to be found now in the stores. Mozzarella cheese comes from Italy and looks like a soft white pillow. Traditionally it is made with buffalo's milk but more readily found made with cow's milk. It is packed in water, which should be drained off before use.

Combined with smoked ham, the turkey escallops and Mozzarella cheese, atop crisp golden croûtes, make a memorable dish. Serve the rich Turkey en Croûtes with a very simple salad of mixed salad greens.

2 large thick slices of fresh bread
2 oz (50g) butter
4–6 medium-sized flat mushrooms
1 tbsp (15ml) flour
Salt and freshly milled pepper
2 turkey escallops about 2 oz (50g) each
2 slices smoked ham
2 oz (50g) Mozzarella cheese
2 tbsp (30ml) chopped parsley

1. Cut each slice of bread into an oval slightly larger than the turkey escallops. Heat one third of the butter in the frypan, slide in the bread and cook over high heat, turning frequently, until golden brown on both sides. Remove and keep hot. Wipe pan with paper towels.
2. Heat half the remaining butter, add the mushrooms and cook over medium heat until soft and brown. Remove with a slotted spoon and keep hot.
3. Season the flour and use to coat the turkey on all sides. Add remaining butter to the pan, add the turkey and cook for about 5 mins. on each side, until golden brown. Remove the pan from the heat.
4. Fold the slices of ham to the size of the turkey escallops and place on top of them. Thinly slice the cheese and cover the ham. Cover the pan and cook

over low heat for 1–2 mins., or until the cheese has melted.

5.   Place each bread croûte on a hot plate and top with a turkey escallop. Add the mushrooms to the side of the plate and sprinkle them with the chopped parsley. Serve immediately.

SPICED DUCK WITH APRICOTS
Serves two   *Takes approx. 25 mins.*

Roast duck is traditionally served with a sweet-sharp sauce such as orange or cherry. This variation uses the plump breast portions, now readily available in packs of two, with a wine and apricot sauce sharpened with a little lemon juice. Ready-to-eat dried apricots are soft and moist and do not need to be soaked before cooking.

Serve the Spiced Duck with lightly cooked whole green beans or sliced courgettes, adding tiny new potatoes or rice if wished.

2 duck breasts
Salt and freshly milled pepper
½ tsp (2.5ml) ground cinnamon
1 tbsp (15ml) oil
1 vegetable stock cube
2 fl oz (50ml) boiling water
¼ pt (150ml) dry white vermouth
3 oz (75g) ready-to-eat dried apricots
2 tbsp (30ml) apricot jam
1 tbsp (15ml) lemon juice

1.   Strip off the skin of the duck breasts if wished. Combine the salt, pepper and cinnamon. Rub into the duck breasts on all sides.
2.   Heat the oil in the frypan, add the duck, skin (or skinned) -side uppermost and cook over medium-high heat, turning frequently, until a rich brown.
3.   Dissolve the stock cube in the water and add to the pan with the vermouth and apricots. Bring just to the boil.

4. Reduce the heat, cover and simmer for 15 mins. or until the duck is just cooked through. Remove the duck from the pan and keep hot.
5. Stir the jam and lemon juice into the wine/stock in the pan, bring to the boil and gently bubble until reduced and beginning to thicken.
6. Cut the duck diagonally across into thin slices. Arrange on hot serving plates and spoon the sauce over, arranging the whole apricots beside the duck. Serve immediately.

6. MAINLY MEAT

BEEF RAGU
Serves two   *Takes approx. 20 mins.*

No self-respecting Italian cook would smother their pasta
with the very rich meat-laden sauces we tend to favour
here. This Italian-inspired sauce relies on the addition of
herbs, red wine and fennel seeds to produce a very full
flavour. The very soft Mozzarella cheese is quite difficult
to grate so I was delighted to find you can now buy it
ready-grated in supermarkets. It melts into soft strings
and has a milder flavour than Parmesan.

Serve the Beef Ragu with spaghetti in shallow bowls,
with a simple green salad and plenty of crusty bread to
mop up the delicious sauce.

1 beef stock cube
¼ pt (150ml) boiling water
¼ pt (150ml) dry red wine
2 tbsp (30ml) tomato paste
1 medium onion
2 sticks celery
2 cloves garlic
2 medium carrots

(continued opposite)

(Beef Ragu continued)

1 tbsp (15ml) olive oil
1 tbsp (15ml) freeze-dried mixed herbs
2 tsp (10ml) sugar
1 tsp (5ml) fennel seeds
½ tsp (2.5ml) ground nutmeg
4 oz (100g) lean minced beef
4–6 oz (100–150g) spaghetti (depending on appetite)
Salt and freshly milled pepper
2 oz (50g) grated Mozzarella cheese

1. Dissolve the stock cube in the water and stir in the wine and tomato paste. Set aside.
2. Peel and finely chop the onion. Thinly slice the celery. Peel and crush the garlic. Scrub or peel the carrots and finely chop.
3. Heat the oil in the frypan and add all the vegetables. Cook, stirring, over medium-high heat until the vegetables are beginning to soften and brown, about 4 mins. Stir in the herbs, sugar, fennel seeds and nutmeg.
4. Add the meat, breaking up any large pieces. Continue to cook until the meat is lightly browned. Pour the stock and wine over it.
5. Bring just to the boil then reduce the heat to medium-low and very gently simmer, stirring occasionally, for about 15 mins. The sauce will thicken slightly and the vegetables soften.
6. While the sauce is simmering cook the pasta according to package directions.
7. Season the sauce with salt and pepper to taste. Drain the pasta and divide between two warm bowls. Spoon the sauce over and sprinkle with the cheese. Serve immediately.

PAN FRIED STEAK WITH GARLICKY MUSHROOMS AND NOODLES

Serves two   *Takes approx. 12 mins.*

Good meat needs only the simplest of treatment to bring out its flavour. Buy the cut of steak you prefer but select a piece that is not too thin – look for one at least 1cm/½ in thick. The thicker the cut, the more succulent it will cook.

Serve the steak and mushrooms with a special salad of crisp lettuce leaves, diced avocado and fresh orange segments lightly tossed with an oil and vinegar dressing.

4 oz (100g) Chinese egg noodles
3 garlic cloves
8 oz (225g) button mushrooms
2 oz (50g) butter
2 steaks, fillet or sirloin
Salt and freshly milled pepper
1 tbsp (15ml) chopped fresh parsley

1. Cook the noodles according to package directions.
2. Peel and crush the garlic. Wipe the mushrooms with a dry cloth and trim the base of each stem. Thickly slice. Set aside.
3. Heat one quarter of the butter in the frypan and slide in the steaks. Cook briefly over high heat just to seal the outside of the meat. Reduce the heat to medium-high and continue to cook until the steak is as well done as you prefer, turning frequently. (Use two spoons to turn steaks to avoid piercing the meat.) As a guide, total cooking time for steak 2cm/¾ in thick: rare 5 mins., medium-rare 9 mins., well-done 12 mins.
4. Remove steaks from pan and keep hot.
5. Heat the remaining butter and stir in the garlic and mushrooms. Cook, stirring, over medium-high heat, until golden brown. Season to taste.
6. Thoroughly drain the noodles and add to the pan. Lightly toss with the mushrooms. Serve with the steaks, pouring the buttery pan juices over the meat. Serve immediately, sprinkled with the parsley.

BEEF AND COCONUT CREAM CURRY
Serves two *Takes approx. 15 mins.*

Absolutely delicious – a dish for a very special meal! Tender strips of beef in a rich coconut cream sauce with just a hint of ginger.

To complete the dish, serve with wild rice. Strictly speaking, wild rice isn't a rice but a grass. The grains are long, thin and dark brown – and very expensive. However, it is now easily available – and affordable – sold mixed with American long grain rice. Cook according to package directions.

Serve the Beef and Coconut Cream Curry with a salad of avocado slices, fresh orange segments and watercress sprigs.

1 in (2.5cm) fresh ginger root
1 large eating apple
1 tbsp (15ml) mild curry sauce
1 vegetable stock cube
¼ pt (150ml) boiling water
¼ pt (150ml) dry white vermouth
1 medium onion
8 oz (225g) sirloin steak
1 tbsp (15ml) oil
2 tsp (10ml) sugar
2 oz (50g) creamed coconut
3 tbsp (45ml) sour cream
Salt and freshly milled pepper

1. Peel and grate the ginger root. Peel, quarter and core the apple. Slice each quarter in half. Whisk together the curry sauce, crumbled stock cube, water and vermouth. Peel and thinly slice the onion. Set aside.
2. Cut the steak across the grain into paper-thin slices. Heat the oil in the frypan, toss in the meat and quickly cook, over medium-high heat, stirring constantly, until brown.
3. Push the meat to one side of the pan and add the onion. Sprinkle it with the sugar and continue to cook until golden brown.
4. Stir in the apple slices and the ginger. Pour the curried

stock over and gently mix the curry together. Cover, reduce the heat to medium and simmer for 10 mins.

5. Chop or grate the creamed coconut and add to the pan. Continue to cook, stirring, until the creamed coconut has dissolved.

6. Stir in the sour cream and season to taste. Serve immediately.

STIR FRIED BEEF IN PINEAPPLE BOATS
Serves two   *Takes approx. 20 mins.*

Tender strips of beef, sweet red pepper and chunks of fresh pineapple in a ginger glaze are spooned back into the pineapple shells in this traditional oriental dish. Serve with chopsticks!

3 tbsp (45ml) dry sherry
3 tbsp (45ml) soy sauce
12 oz (350g) sirloin steak
1 in (2.5cm) fresh ginger root
1 small ripe pineapple
1 medium red pepper
4 spring onions
2 tsp (10ml) cornflour
2 tbsp (30ml) oil
Salt and freshly milled pepper

1. Combine 15ml/1 tbsp each of the sherry and soy sauce in a shallow bowl. Very thinly slice the steak across the grain. Add to the bowl and mix well. Leave to marinate while preparing the other ingredients.

2. Grate the ginger root into a small bowl, add the remaining sherry and soy sauce. Set aside.

3. Carefully cut the pineapple in half from top to bottom, right through the leaves, to give two matching halves. Using a small knife cut out the flesh, leaving the skins whole. Cut the flesh into chunks, set the skins aside.

4. Halve the pepper, discarding the stem, seeds and

pith. Cut into strips. Cut the spring onions across diagonally into 5cm/2 in slices.
5. Drain the meat, sprinkle it with the cornflour and mix well together – easiest using your fingers. Separate the slices.
6. Heat the oil in the frypan until sizzling, toss in the meat and cook, stirring, over high heat until brown. Remove with a slotted spoon.
7. Add the pepper strips and spring onions to the pan and cook until just tender – about 1 min. Add the pineapple chunks, pour the ginger-sherry mixture over and continue to cook, stirring, until the glaze thickens slightly. Season to taste.
8. Add the beef, lightly toss together, spoon into the pineapple shells and serve immediately.

CANTONESE PORK
Serves two   *Takes approx. 10 mins.*

A very quick stir fry of thinly sliced lean pork, pineapple and cashew nuts in a slightly sweet-sour sauce.

The recipe makes two very generous servings so only a simple salad such as wedges of iceberg lettuce with mayonnaise may be needed. For heartier appetites serve quickly prepared egg noodles or freshly cooked rice.

227g can pineapple slices in juice
3 tbsp (45ml) white wine vinegar
2 tbsp (30ml) soft brown sugar
2 tbsp (30ml) soy sauce
1 vegetable stock cube
Salt and freshly milled pepper
1 tbsp (15ml) cornflour
1 small green pepper
4 young carrots
4 sticks celery
4 spring onions
2 oz (50g) cashew nuts
8 oz (225g) pork fillet
1 tbsp (15ml) oil

1. Drain the pineapple juice into a measuring jug and make up to 8 fl oz (225ml) with cold water. Add the vinegar, sugar, soy sauce, crumbled stock cube and salt and pepper. Whisk in the cornflour and set aside. Cut each pineapple slice into eight and set aside.
2. Halve the pepper lengthwise, discarding the stem, pith and seeds. Cut the flesh into small strips. Scrub or peel the carrots and cut into matchsticks. Thinly slice the celery. Trim and diagonally cut the onions into 1 in/2.5cm pieces. Add the carrots, celery and onions to the pepper and set aside.
3. Tip the cashews into the frypan and cook, stirring, over medium-high heat until golden brown. (No need to use any oil.) Remove from the pan.
4. Cut the pork into paper-thin slices. Heat the oil in the frypan and add the pork. Cook, stirring constantly, over high heat until golden brown.
5. Add the vegetables and continue to cook, stirring, until just beginning to soften – about 3 mins.
6. Whisk the pineapple juice mixture (cornflour has a habit of falling to the bottom of the jug) and pour over the pork and vegetables. Add the pineapple pieces and the nuts and bring just to the boil.
7. Continue to cook, stirring, until the glaze has thickened.
8. Serve immediately.

PORK AND POTATO PAN FRY
Serves two *Takes approx. 30 mins.*

Meat, potatoes and gravy all in one pan. Choose pork chops with or without the bone and cut about ¾ in/2cm thick so that they remain moist when cooked. Trim off any excess fat.

Serve with a lightly cooked green vegetable such as Brussels sprouts or with a simple green salad.

1 medium onion
1 vegetable stock cube
5 fl oz (150ml) boiling water
2 large potatoes
2 tbsp (30ml) oil
2 tsp (10ml) sugar
2 pork chops
4 tbsp (60ml) dry sherry
Salt and freshly milled pepper

1. Peel and thinly slice the onion. Dissolve the stock cube in the boiling water. Set aside. Peel the potatoes and cut into slices about ¼ in/½cm thick.
2. Heat half the oil in the frypan and add half the potato slices in a single layer. Cook over medium-high heat, turning once or twice, until just golden brown on both sides. Remove from the pan and repeat with remaining oil and potato slices. Remove from the pan.
3. Add the onion to the pan and sprinkle with the sugar. Cook, stirring, for a minute or two then push the onion to the side of the pan and add the chops.
4. Pressing the chops down onto the pan surface, cook until well browned on both sides.
5. Add the sherry and stock and lightly season with salt and pepper. Arrange the potato slices on top of the chops.
6. Cover and reduce the heat to a gentle simmer. Cook until the chops are tender, 15–20 mins. Do not cook too fast as this will toughen the chops.
7. Serve each chop with half the potatoes and the gravy.

GINGERED PORK AND CABBAGE
Serves two   *Takes approx. 10 mins.*

Tender shreds of pork, coated with ground ginger and soy
sauce, lightly stir fried with leeks and slivered cabbage and
sprinkled with crunchy sunflower seeds. If possible, mix
the pork with the marinade about 20 mins. before cooking
to allow the flavours to blend with the meat. In place of
the pork, both lamb fillet or chicken breast meat is equally
good.

Serve with a crisp salad of very thinly sliced sweet-
flavoured red and yellow peppers tossed with olive oil,
lemon juice and seasonings.

1½ tsp (7.5ml) ground ginger
2 tsp (10ml) soft brown sugar
2 tbsp (30ml) dry white vermouth
4 tbsp (60ml) soy sauce
12 oz (350g) pork fillet
1 small leek OR 4 spring onions
8 oz (225g) wedge Savoy cabbage
4 oz (100g) Chinese egg noodles
3 tbsp (45ml) sunflower seeds
1 tbsp (15ml) oil
Salt and freshly milled pepper

1. Combine the ground ginger, sugar, vermouth and soy
    sauce in a shallow dish. Slice the pork fillet diagonally
    into paper-thin slices. Add to the ginger mixture and
    work well together with your fingers. Set aside.
2. Trim and clean the leek (or spring onions) and very
    thinly slice. VERY finely shred the cabbage, discard-
    ing the stem and any thick parts of the leaves. Add to
    the leek (or onions) and set aside.
3. Cook the noodles according to package directions.
4. Toss the sunflower seeds (without oil) into the frypan
    and cook, stirring constantly, over medium-high heat
    until golden brown. Tip out onto paper towel.
5. Heat the oil in the frypan. Using a slotted spoon, lift
    the meat from the marinade and add to the pan.
    Cook, stirring constantly, over medium-high heat for
    3 mins.

6. Add the leek (or onions) and cabbage and continue to cook, stirring constantly, for 2–3 mins. until vegetables are just tender.
7. Pour any remaining marinade over and season to taste.
8. Drain the noodles, add to the pan and toss to mix. Cook, stirring, for 1 min. to heat through then serve immediately, sprinkled with the sunflower seeds.

GLAZED BACON CHOPS WITH BUTTER BEANS
Serves two   *Takes approx. 12 mins.*

Inexpensive bacon chops taste extra good coated with an apricot, clove and lemon glaze and gently simmered with butter beans. Both gammon steaks and pork chops are equally good cooked this way. Allow a little longer cooking time for thick pork chops.

Served with the butter beans, the Glazed Bacon Chops make a generous meal. Serve with a simple green salad and crusty bread to mop up the sauce.

1 medium onion
3 tbsp (45ml) apricot jam
2 tbsp (30ml) lemon juice
1 tsp (5ml) ground cloves
1 vegetable stock cube
3 fl oz (75ml) boiling water
1 medium eating apple
2 thick-cut bacon chops
1 oz (25g) butter
15.2 oz (432g) can butter beans

1. Peel and thinly slice the onion. Stir together the jam, lemon juice, cloves, crumbled stock cube and boiling water. Set aside.
2. Cut a thin slice from the top and bottom of the apple and discard. Remove the core and cut the apple into four slices. Heat half the butter in the frypan and add

the apple slices. Cook over medium-high heat, turning frequently, until golden brown on both sides.
Remove from the pan and keep hot.

3.   Scissor-snip the fat edge of the bacon chops two or
three times to prevent them curling. Place the chops
in the hot pan and cook until well browned on both
sides. Remove from the pan.

4.   Melt remaining butter in the pan and stir in the onion.
Cook, stirring, until soft but not brown. Add the
apricot jam mixture and bring just to the boil.

5.   Drain the beans and add to the pan. Return the bacon
chops to the pan, turning to coat with the glaze. Top
each chop with two apple slices.

6.   Cover the pan, reduce the heat to medium and cook
for a further 5 mins. Serve immediately.

LIVER OPORTO
Serves two   *Takes approx. 15 mins.*

Even the most determined liver haters may well enjoy this
delicious way of cooking something that really is good for
you! Take care to cook the liver just lightly or it will
become dry and tough. If fresh sage is not to hand use
dried mixed herbs. Don't be tempted to leave out the
olives – they add a piquant salty tang to the dish.
Serve Liver Oporto with mashed potatoes or rice.

12 oz (350g) lamb's liver
3 tbsp (45ml) milk
2 tbsp (30ml) flour
1 large onion
1 tbsp (15ml) oil
8.1 oz (230g) can chopped tomatoes
2 tbsp (30ml) dry sherry
2 tbsp (30ml) tomato ketchup
2 tsp (10ml) chopped fresh sage
Salt and freshly ground pepper
2 oz (50g) black olives

1. Liver is often sold ready sliced. If not, peel off any outer membrane and cut out any internal ducts. Cut into very thin slices.
2. Dip each slice into the milk, then lightly coat with flour.
3. Peel and thinly slice the onion. Heat the oil in the frypan and add the onion. Cook over medium heat, stirring frequently, until soft and just beginning to brown.
4. Add the slices of liver, increase the heat and cook, stirring, until they just start to brown.
5. Add the canned tomatoes, sherry, ketchup and herb.
6. Bring just to the boil and stir to blend together. Reduce the heat and gently cook for 5 mins., stirring frequently.
7. Season to taste and add the olives.
8. Serve immediately.

PAPRIKA SAUSAGE
Serves two *Takes approx. 15 mins.*

A budget special; for very hungry appetites use one pound (450g) sausage meat. Omit the mushrooms if preferred.

Serve the Sausage Paprika with jacket or mashed potatoes, or if that takes too long, slip the sausage cakes inside large soft baps and top with the paprika sauce and a spoonful of yoghurt.

1 medium onion
2 oz (50g) button mushrooms (optional)
1 tbsp (15ml) plain flour
1 tsp (5ml) freeze-dried mixed herbs
Salt and freshly milled pepper
12 oz (350g) good quality pork sausage meat
2 tsp (10ml) oil
8.1 oz (230g) can chopped tomatoes
1 tbsp (15ml) tomato purée
2 tsp (10ml) paprika
2 tsp (10ml) sugar
2 tsp (10ml) red wine vinegar
4 tbsp (60ml) natural yoghurt

1. Peel and finely chop the onion. Wipe, trim and slice the mushrooms. Set aside.
2. Combine the flour, herbs and seasoning on a sheet of greaseproof paper. Divide the sausage meat into four slices and shape into neat cakes. Coat with the seasoned flour.
3. Heat one teaspoonful of the oil in the frypan and add the sausage cakes. Cook over medium-high heat until golden brown on both sides. Remove from the pan.
4. Add the remaining oil to the pan and stir in the onion. Cook, stirring, until soft but not brown. Add the mushrooms and continue to cook, stirring, until they begin to brown.
5. Stir in the tomatoes, tomato purée, paprika, sugar and vinegar. Bring just to the boil, stir well and season to taste.
6. Return the sausage cakes to the pan. Cook over medium heat for 10 mins., turning the sausage cakes over once or twice. Serve immediately as suggested above, topping each sausage cake with a spoonful of yoghurt.

SMOKED SAUSAGE SUPPER
Serves two   *Takes approx. 25 mins.*

Very quickly prepared, this filling supper is ideal for a busy day – cook on a low heat and it will happily simmer gently without frequent attention. You will find concentrated apple juice in healthfood shops. Keep in the fridge once opened, it is very useful for sweetening both savoury and fruit dishes. For a change use meaty pork or beef sausages instead of the smoked sausage and cook them in the frypan before starting the recipe. Remove from the pan and keep warm. Continue the recipe as below, replacing the sausages in step 6.

Serve the Sausage Supper with chunks of warm granary bread.

8 oz (225g) red cabbage
1 medium cooking apple
1 medium onion
1 tsp (5ml) oil
1 tbsp (15ml) red wine vinegar
2 tbsp (30ml) clear honey
2 tbsp (30ml) concentrated apple juice
½ tsp (2.5ml) ground cloves
5 fl oz (150ml) cold water
Salt and freshly milled pepper
8 oz (225g) smoked sausage

1. Remove the centre stalk and very finely shred the cabbage, discarding any tough parts. Set aside. Peel, core and thinly slice the apple and add to the cabbage.
2. Peel and thinly slice the onion. Heat the oil in the frypan, add the onion, cover and cook until soft, stirring once or twice – about 3 mins. Remove from the heat.
3. Stir in the cabbage and apple.
4. Combine the vinegar, honey, apple juice, cloves and water and add to the pan.
5. Bring to the boil, stirring. Cover and simmer gently for 10 mins. or until cabbage is almost cooked, stirring once or twice. Season to taste.
6. Halve the sausage, removing the skin if wished. Add to the pan, pushing it down into the vegetables.
7. Cover and continue to simmer for 10 mins., turning the sausage over once.
8. Spoon the cabbage onto two warm plates and arrange a portion of sausage on top of each. Serve at once.

LAMB STEAKS AND RICE WITH GINGER-LIME GLAZE

Serves two   *Takes approx. 25 mins.*

Look for boneless leg of lamb steaks or use noisettes, the boned chops tied into neat round shapes. Allow 4–6 oz (100–175g) per person. If you use Basmati rice, rinse in a sieve under cold running water before use. Alternatively, use long grain white rice. No limes? Use a lemon – different but just as good!

Serve with Naan (or Nan) bread, a soft irregular-shaped bread from India and now sold in our supermarkets. If possible, lightly grill on both sides before serving. A simple salad of very thinly sliced cucumber and spring onions sprinkled with salt and pepper gives a crisp cool contrast to the rich meat and rice.

1 medium onion
1 large lime
1 in (2.5cm) fresh ginger root
2 tbsp (30ml) clear honey
2 vegetable stock cubes
¾ pt (450ml) boiling water
1 tbsp (15ml) oil
2 boneless leg of lamb steaks or noisettes (see above)
4 oz (100g) Basmati rice
¼ pt (150ml) natural yoghurt
Salt and freshly milled pepper

1. Peel and thinly slice the onion. Finely grate the lime rind and extract the juice. Grate the ginger root and combine with the lime rind and juice, and the honey. Dissolve the stock cubes in the boiling water. Set aside.
2. Heat the oil in the frypan and stir in the onion slices. Cook, stirring, over medium heat until soft and beginning to brown.
3. Push the onion to the side of the pan and add the lamb steaks (or noisettes). Pressing down onto the surface of the pan, cook until browned on both sides.
4. Pour over the lime-ginger mixture and turn the meat to coat on both sides.

5.   Spoon the rice around the lamb and pour the stock over. Bring just to the boil then reduce the heat to a gentle simmer. Cover and cook until the rice has absorbed the stock, about 12 mins.
6.   Meanwhile, season the yoghurt with salt and pepper and stir well. Serve with the lamb and rice.

LAMB WITH MINTED BARLEY
Serves two   *Takes approx. 25 mins.*

Tender lean fillets of lamb are first lightly browned, then gently cooked with barley, leeks and carrots to make a very satisfying dish. Remember to use the widely available 'easy-cook' pearl barley which reduces the cooking time.

Serve with a tossed salad of watercress sprigs, thinly sliced celery, diced cucumber and fresh grapefruit segments.

1 chicken stock cube
½ pt (300ml) boiling water
1 lemon
2 small leeks
2 medium carrots
12 oz (350g) lean lamb fillet
1 tsp (5ml) oil
3 oz (75g) 'easy-cook' pearl barley
Salt and freshly milled pepper
1 tbsp (15ml) chopped parsley
1 tbsp (15ml) chopped mint
Mint sprigs for garnish

1.   Dissolve the stock cube in the water. Finely grate the lemon rind and extract the juice. Add both to the stock. Set aside.
2.   Trim the leeks and halve lengthwise. Thoroughly rinse under running water to remove any grit and drain well. Cut into 1 in/2.5cm slices. Scrub or peel the carrots. Cut in quarters lengthwise and then across in ½ in/1cm slices. Set aside.

3. Remove any excess fat from the lamb fillet and cut
    across into two portions. Using a very sharp knife,
    lightly score the surface on both sides. This keeps the
    meat flat when cooking.
4. Heat the oil in the frypan and add the lamb. Cook
    over medium-high heat, turning frequently, until
    golden brown on both sides. Remove from the pan.
5. Off the heat, add the vegetables, pearl barley and
    stock to the pan. Return to the heat and bring just to
    the boil.
6. Return the lamb to the pan, cover and simmer gently
    for 20 mins. or until the barley is tender and has
    absorbed the stock.
7. Lift out the lamb and cut each portion into thin slices.
    Arrange on warm plates. Season the barley to taste
    and stir in the parsley and mint. Spoon onto the plates
    beside the lamb. Serve immediately garnished with
    the mint sprigs.

PEPPERED LAMB-BURGERS
Serves two   *Takes approx. 20 mins.*

Minced lamb may be found in most supermarkets but
minced beef or pork could be used instead. Only brown
the lamb-burgers in step 2 and complete their cooking in
the sauce in step 6. This keeps them tender and moist.

Serve Peppered Lamb-Burgers with hot French bread
or freshly cooked rice.

1 small onion
1 green pepper
1 red pepper
4 oz (100g) button mushrooms
12 oz (350g) minced lamb
1 oz (25g) butter
1 tbsp (15ml) plain flour
1 tsp (5ml) paprika
2 fl oz (50ml) milk
5 fl oz (150ml) sour cream
Salt and freshly milled pepper

1. Peel and thinly slice the onion. Separate into rings and set aside. Thinly slice both peppers into rings, discarding the stem, seeds and any pith. Add to the onion. Slice the mushrooms if large.
2. Divide the minced lamb into two portions and lightly shape with wet fingers into two flat, but not too thin, ovals. Melt half the butter in the frypan, slip in the lamb-burgers and cook, carefully turning once or twice until just golden brown. Remove from the pan with a slotted spoon and set aside.
3. Melt the remaining butter in the pan and add the onion and peppers. Cook, stirring, for 5 mins. Add the mushrooms and continue to cook for a further 3 mins.
4. Sprinkle the flour and paprika over and stir in, cooking for 1 min.
5. Remove from the heat and add the milk and sour cream. Cook, stirring, until the sauce thickens and just comes to the boil. Season to taste.
6. Push the vegetables to the side of the pan and place the lamb-burgers in the centre. Reduce the heat to a gentle simmer, cover and cook for 5 mins. longer or until the lamb-burgers are just cooked.
7. Place a lamb-burger on each warm plate and spoon the sauce over the top.

7. VEGETARIAN DELIGHTS

SMOKY TOFU PAELLA
Serves two   *Takes approx. 20 mins.*

Even the most dedicated meat eater will not notice the absence of the traditional chicken, sausage and seafood ingredients in this very delicious version of the Spanish dish. It is a feast to the eye and the taste-buds!

A simple salad of peeled, thinly sliced oranges and sweet red onions sprinkled with a little oil and vinegar dressing is all that is needed to complete the meal.

Half a yellow pepper
Half a red pepper
2 oz (50g) French beans
2 ripe tomatoes
Boiling water
2 vegetable stock cubes
One lemon
Pinch saffron threads
220g pack smoked tofu
1 medium onion
1 clove garlic
1 tbsp (15ml) olive oil

(continued opposite)

(Smoky Tofu Paella continued)

4 oz (100g) long grain rice
2 oz (50g) frozen peas
2 oz (50g) black olives

1. Cut the peppers into strips discarding stem, seeds and any pith. 'Top and tail' the beans and cut into 1 in/ 2.5cm pieces. Slash the skin of the tomatoes at the stem end and cover with boiling water. Leave for 1 min. Drain, peel off the skins and cut into quarters, removing the seeds if wished. Set aside.
2. Crumble the stock cubes into ¾ pt (450ml) boiling water. Cut the lemon in half and squeeze the juice from one half, reserving the other for a garnish. Add the lemon juice and saffron to the stock. Dry the tofu on paper towel and cut into 1 in/2.5cm cubes. Set aside.
3. Peel and thinly slice the onion. Peel and crush the garlic.
4. Heat the oil in the frypan and add the tofu cubes. Cook, over medium-high heat until golden brown, gently turning to avoid breaking it up. Remove with a slotted spoon.
5. Add the onion and garlic to the pan. Cook, stirring, until soft and beginning to brown. Add the peppers and cook until they begin to soften.
6. Stir in the rice. Add the saffron stock and the beans. Bring just to the boil, cover and reduce the heat to a very gentle simmer. Cook for 12–15 mins. or until the rice is tender.
7. Gently blend in the tomatoes, peas and olives. Continue to cook for a few minutes until the peas are hot. Carefully stir in the tofu. Cover and remove from the heat. Allow to stand for 2–3 mins.
8. Pile onto warm plates and garnish with the remaining half of the lemon, cut into wedges. Serve immediately.

PEPPERED BEAN TACOS

Serves two   *Takes approx. 30 mins,*
                                          incl. 15 mins soaking.

The packs of cereal, soya and vegetable mix are a useful
store cupboard stand-by, needing only to be mixed with
water (and an egg, depending on the brand purchased)
and allowed to rehydrate. Then shape into balls, sausages
or burgers and cook.

No taco shells? Spoon the Peppered Beans into split
pitta breads or soft baps.

**1 pack soya-based vegetable sausage mix, approx. 4 oz
    (125g) size
1 egg (if needed – see method)
1 medium onion
1 clove garlic
3 sticks celery
2 oz (50g) vegetarian Cheddar cheese
Small wedge firm lettuce
1 tbsp (15ml) oil
15.7 oz (447g) can mixed beans in spicy pepper sauce
1 packet Mexican taco shells**

1. Prepare the sausage mix according to package direc-
    tions, adding an egg if required. Leave to rehydrate
    while preparing the other ingredients.
2. Peel and finely chop the onion. Peel and crush the
    garlic. Very finely slice the celery. Add the garlic and
    celery to the onion. Grate the cheese and finely shred
    the lettuce. Set aside.
3. Using lightly floured fingers, divide and shape the
    sausage mix into approximately 16 small balls. Heat
    the oil in the frypan, add the balls and fry, gently
    stirring, until a deep golden brown on all sides.
    Remove from the pan with a slotted spoon.
4. Add the onion, garlic and celery to the pan. Cook,
    stirring, over medium-high heat, until soft. Add the
    beans and continue to cook until bubbling hot. Return
    the balls to the pan and stir in.
5. Serve spooned into the taco shells or pitta breads and
    top with finely shredded lettuce and grated cheese.
    Serve immediately.

MUSHROOM AND WHEAT PILAFF
Serves two   *Takes approx. 14 mins.*

Bulgar wheat (spelt various ways including Bulghur or Burghul) is produced from whole wheat grains which have been steamed, dried and then processed into small pieces. It can be eaten simply soaked as in the Lebanese salad Tabbouleh or very quickly cooked with other ingredients as in this recipe.

Serve with a simple crisp green salad with a sliced green-skinned eating apple added to it.

1 large onion
2 cloves garlic
6 oz (175g) button mushrooms
1 tbsp (15ml) olive oil
4 oz (100g) hazelnuts
1 tsp (5ml) sugar
2 vegetable stock cubes
¾ pt (450ml) boiling water
4 oz (100g) bulgar wheat
Salt and pepper
4 tbsp (60ml) sour cream
Paprika

1. Peel and thinly slice the onion. Peel and crush the garlic. Wipe and slice the mushrooms.
2. Heat the oil in the frypan and add the onion, garlic, mushrooms and hazelnuts. Sprinkle with the sugar. Cook, stirring, over medium-high heat until a rich golden brown. Remove from the heat.
3. Dissolve the stock cubes in the water and add to the pan with the wheat. Stir well and bring just to the boil.
4. Cover and reduce the heat to low. Gently simmer for 8–10 mins. or until the wheat has absorbed all the stock.
5. Season to taste.
6. Serve on warm plates, spooning the sour cream on top. Sprinkle with a little paprika and serve immediately.

CHICKPEA AND BARLEY PILAFF

Serves two   *Takes approx. 22 mins.*

Pearl barley makes an interesting change from rice as the basis of pilaff but, until recently, took rather a long time to cook. Now, with packets of an 'easy cook' variety available the cooking time is reduced to about twenty minutes. Tip the unused half of the can of chickpeas into a small container, cover and keep in the fridge – do not leave in the opened can. Use within two days, in another recipe or add to a salad.

Combined with chickpeas and pinenuts this is a very satisfying dish. Serve with a plate of crudités – raw vegetables cut into attractive pieces, such as carrot and celery sticks, red and yellow pepper rings – and cherry tomatoes plus a bowl of garlic mayonnaise as a 'serve yourself' salad.

2 vegetable stock cubes
1 pt (600ml) boiling water
1 lemon
2 tbsp (30ml) soy sauce
2 oz (50g) pinenuts
4 oz (100g) 'easy cook' pearl barley
Half a 15.2 oz (432g) can chickpeas
Salt and freshly milled pepper

1. Crumble the stock cubes into the water. Finely grate the lemon rind and extract the juice. Add both plus 1 tbsp (15ml) soy sauce to the stock. Set aside.
2. Tip the pinenuts into the frypan and cook, stirring, over medium-high heat until golden brown. Sprinkle with the remaining soy sauce, stir well then tip out of the pan onto a plate. Set aside.
3. Add the pearl barley to the pan with the stock. Bring just to the boil, stir and cover. Reduce the heat to low and gently simmer for 15 mins.
4. Drain the can of chickpeas and add the half to the pan. Continue to cook for 5 mins. longer or until the barley is tender and has absorbed all the stock.
5. Season to taste and spoon onto hot plates. Sprinkle with the pinenuts and serve immediately.

PESTO BEANS WITH VEGETABLE SAUSAGES

Serves two
Takes approx. 10 mins., plus 15 mins. to allow sausage mix to soak

A new twist to 'Bangers-and-Beans'! Pretty pale green flageolet beans in a basil and sour cream sauce, served with 'sausages' made from a soy-based vegetable sausage mix. This inexpensive mix needs only to be mixed with water (plus an egg depending on which brand you buy) and allowed to rehydrate before shaping into rolls or balls. They have a good savoury flavour but I personally like to serve them in a sauce as in this recipe.

Pesto is a rich Italian sauce made of basil, pinenuts, Parmesan cheese and olive oil. Look for the little jars among the pasta sauces in the Italian section of your supermarket. After opening, store in the fridge. To avoid it growing 'whiskers', after use level the top with a teaspoon and carefully wipe any pesto from the neck of the bottle with paper towel. Pour in a very thin layer of olive oil. This makes an airtight seal on top of the pesto extending its keeping qualities. Stir before using again.

This recipe makes two generous servings, needing only crusty rolls and a sliced tomato salad to make a satisfying meal.

1 pack soya-based vegetable sausage mix, approx. 4 oz
        (125g) size
1 egg (if needed – see method)
1 vegetable stock cube
3 fl oz (75ml) boiling water
1 medium onion
3 tbsp (45ml) pesto
¼ pt (150ml) sour cream
14.5 oz (410g) can flageolet beans
1 tbsp (15ml) oil
Salt and freshly milled pepper
Paprika

1. Prepare the sausage mix according to package directions, adding an egg if required. Leave to rehydrate

while preparing other ingredients.

2. Dissolve the stock cube in the water. Peel and thinly slice the onion. Stir the pesto into the sour cream. Drain the beans. Set aside.

3. With lightly wetted fingers divide the sausage mix into four portions and shape each into an oval.

4. Heat the oil in the frypan, slip in the 'sausages' and cook over medium-high heat, turning once or twice until golden brown on both sides. Remove with a slotted spoon and keep warm.

5. Add the onion to the pan and cook, stirring, for 1–2 mins. until soft. Add the stock and beans, cover and reduce the heat to medium. Simmer for 5 mins.

6. Stir in the pesto and sour cream and return the 'sausages' to the pan. Cover and simmer for a further 5 mins. Season to taste and serve immediately, sprinkled with a little paprika.

VEGETABLE RAGOUT
Serves two   *Takes approx. 15 mins.*

A colourful selection of vegetables in a mild chilli and apple flavoured sauce. When courgettes are unavailable, use button mushrooms, cauliflower sprigs or sliced carrots. Cook the vegetables just until tender, not too soft. Add extra chilli sauce for a hotter flavour.

Serve the Ragout in shallow bowls with lots of hot garlic or herbed bread (add chopped herbs to the butter instead of crushed garlic).

1 medium onion
2 cloves garlic
12 oz (350g) young courgettes
1 red pepper
2 tsp (10ml) cornflour
3 tbsp (45ml) concentrated apple juice
2 tbsp (30ml) chilli sauce
Cold water
2 large slices fresh bread
2 oz (50g) butter

(continued opposite)

(Vegetable Ragout continued)

Salt and freshly milled pepper
4 eggs, hard-boiled

1. Peel and thinly slice the onion. Peel and crush the garlic and add to the onion. Set aside. Wash and trim the courgettes. Cut into ½ in/1cm slices. Cut the pepper in half lengthwise, discarding the stem, seeds and any white pith. Cut into 1 in/2.5cm squares. Add to the courgettes and set aside.
2. Add the cornflour to the apple juice in a measuring jug. Whisk until smooth then stir in the chilli sauce. Make up to 7 fl oz/200ml with cold water and stir well. Set aside.
3. Cut off the crusts and make the bread into crumbs in a processor or with a grater.
4. Heat half the butter in the frypan and stir in the crumbs. Cook, stirring constantly, over medium-high heat until golden brown. Remove from the pan onto a plate. Keep hot.
5. Add the remaining butter to the pan and stir in the onion and garlic. Cook, stirring, over medium-high heat until just soft but not brown.
6. Tip in the courgettes and pepper. Cook, stirring, until just tender. Stir the cornflour mixture and add to the pan. Continue to cook, stirring, until the sauce comes to the boil, is thickened and smooth. Season to taste.
7. Spoon into heated bowls and top with the buttered crumbs. Shell and quarter the eggs and arrange around the edge. Serve immediately.

SMOKED TOFU STIR FRY
Serves two   *Takes approx. 10 mins.*

Tofu is made from soya beans and is a high quality protein widely used in vegetarian and oriental cookery. It is sold in several forms from very soft (silken tofu) to the firm cheese-like type used in this recipe. In plain form it is very bland but I think the smoked variety has a delicious flavour. It is an inexpensive, low fat form of protein well worth trying. It is sold chilled in supermarkets and wholefood stores and should be kept refrigerated.

This recipe makes two generous servings. Finish the meal with chilled fresh satsumas or oranges.

4 oz (100g) egg noodles
4 spring onions
4 oz (100g) mangetout
2 young carrots
1 in (2.5cm) fresh ginger root
1 clove garlic
3 tbsp (45ml) soy sauce
2 tbsp (30ml) dry sherry
2 tsp (10ml) cornflour
2 tbsp (30ml) cold water
Salt and freshly milled pepper
8 oz (225g) smoked tofu
1 tbsp (15ml) oil
4 oz (100g) beansprouts
2 tbsp (30ml) sunflower seeds

1. Cook the egg noodles according to package directions.
2. Trim the spring onions and cut diagonally into 1 in/ 2.5cm slices. 'Top and tail' the mangetout. Scrub or peel the carrots and cut into matchstick-sized pieces. Set the vegetables aside.
3. Peel and grate the ginger root. Peel and crush the garlic. Add both to the soy sauce and sherry in a small bowl. Mix the cornflour to a cream with the water and add to the soy sauce mixture. Season with salt and pepper.
4. Dry the tofu on paper towel and cut into 1 in/2.5cm cubes. Heat the oil in the frypan, add the tofu and cook, stirring, for 2 mins. Remove with a slotted spoon.
5. Add the spring onions, mangetout and carrots to the frypan. Cook, stirring, for 3 mins. Add the bean-sprouts and continue to cook, stirring, for 2 mins.
6. Pour the soy sauce mixture over and cook, stirring, just until the glaze has thickened and coated the vegetables.
7. Gently stir in the tofu and the well drained noodles.
8. Spoon on to warm plates and sprinkle with the sunflower seeds. Serve immediately.

VEGETABLE SATAY

Serves two   *Takes approx. 20 mins.*

The Indonesian dish called Satay (or Saté) is traditionally meat or poultry cooked on wooden skewers and served with a peanut-based sauce. This adaptation uses a selection of vegetables cooked with a peanut butter and chilli glaze, served with a cool yoghurt and cucumber sauce. Use new or salad potatoes as they will not break up when cooking.

I find a simple salad of lettuce and diced avocado goes well with the Vegetable Satay, and wedges of fresh pineapple to follow complete the Indonesian theme.

6 in (15cm) piece cucumber
4 tbsp (60ml) crunchy peanut butter
2 tbsp (30ml) soy sauce
1 tsp (5ml) chilli powder
1 tbsp (15ml) soft brown sugar
Half a lemon
1 vegetable stock cube
½ pt (300ml) boiling water
12 oz (350g) new or salad potatoes
6 oz (175g) young courgettes
1 medium onion
2 cloves garlic
1 tbsp (15ml) oil
Salt and freshly milled pepper
¼ pt (150ml) natural yoghurt

1. Finely dice the cucumber and place in a small bowl. Combine the peanut butter with the soy sauce, chilli powder, sugar and the juice of the lemon half. Dissolve the stock cube in the water. Set all aside.
2. Scrub the potatoes and cut into bite-sized pieces. Wash and trim the courgettes. Cut into ½ in/1cm slices. Peel and thinly slice the onion. Peel and crush the garlic.
3. Heat the oil in the frypan and add the onion and garlic. Cook, stirring, over medium-high heat until soft and just beginning to brown. Stir in the potatoes and cook for 1–2 mins.

4. Pour the stock over, cover and reduce the heat to medium. Cook, stirring once or twice, for 10 mins. Stir in the courgettes, cover and continue to cook until both vegetables are tender.
5. Gently stir in the peanut butter glaze and cook just until bubbling hot. Remove from the heat and season to taste.
6. Add the yoghurt to the cucumber and season to taste.
7. Spoon the Vegetable Satay onto hot plates and add the cucumber-yoghurt sauce to one side. Serve immediately.

SESAME POTATOES
Serves two   *Takes approx. 15 mins.*

Tahini paste, found in healthfood stores, is made of crushed sesame seed and provides a very good, versatile source of protein in non-meat meals. It is a main ingredient of hummus, the chickpea pâté and may be used in salad dressings. I like it combined with yoghurt and used as a dressing over freshly cooked vegetables. Tiny new potatoes, now available all the year round, are gently simmered in stock before adding the sesame sauce. Try other vegetables too, such as cauliflower or parsnips.

Serve the Sesame Potatoes with a salad of finely shredded lettuce topped with sliced tomatoes, spring onions and oil and vinegar dressing.

¼ pt (150ml) natural yoghurt
3 tbsp (45ml) tahini paste
2 tsp (10ml) cornflour
Half a lemon
2 tbsp (30ml) finely chopped parsley
Salt and freshly milled pepper
1 vegetable stock cube
½ pt (300ml) boiling water
12 oz (350g) tiny new potatoes
2 cloves garlic

(continued opposite)

(Sesame Potatoes continued)

1 medium onion
1 tbsp (15ml) olive oil
2 eggs, freshly hard-boiled

1. Whisk together the yoghurt, tahini paste and corn-
    flour. Squeeze the juice from the lemon and add to
    the yoghurt. Stir in the parsley and seasoning.
    Dissolve the stock cube in the water. Set aside.
2. Scrub the potatoes. Peel and crush the garlic. Peel
    and thinly slice the onion.
3. Heat the oil in the frypan and add the garlic, onion
    and potatoes. Cook over medium-high heat, stirring,
    for 3–4 mins. until beginning to brown.
4. Add the stock, cover and reduce the heat to a gentle
    simmer. Cook until the potatoes are just tender.
5. Uncover, increase the heat and continue to cook until
    the stock has almost evaporated. Stir in the tahini-
    yoghurt mixture and continue to cook, stirring, until
    bubbling hot.
6. Spoon onto hot plates and add a shelled, halved egg
    to each. Serve immediately.

KASHMIRI QUORN
Serves two   *Takes approx. 14 mins.*

Quorn is a versatile alternative to meat, harvested from a
tiny plant related to the mushroom. Quorn has the texture
of meat and a light savoury taste, is an excellent source of
protein and fibre yet is very low in fat. It can be bought
chilled or frozen and is very good value as there is no
wastage at all. In Kashmiri Quorn it is cooked in a mild
curry sauce flavoured with coconut plus apple and banana
chunks to add sweetness.
    Serve with warm Naan breads and a simple green salad.

1 vegetable stock cube
½ pt (300ml) boiling water
2 oz (50g) creamed coconut

(continued overleaf)

(Kashmiri Quorn continued)

1 red-skinned eating apple
1 medium onion
3 sticks celery
1 tbsp (15ml) oil
2 tsp (10ml) sugar
2 tbsp (30ml) tomato purée
2 tbsp (30ml) curry sauce
8 oz (225g) pack Quorn, thawed if frozen
1 large banana
2 tbsp (30ml) mango chutney
Salt and freshly milled pepper

1. Dissolve the stock cube in the water. Dice the coconut. Quarter, core and cut the apple into thick slices. Set aside.
2. Peel and thinly slice the onion. Thinly slice the celery. Heat the oil in the frypan and stir in the onion, celery and apple. Sprinkle with the sugar and cook, stirring, over medium-high heat until pale golden brown. Remove from the heat.
3. Add the stock, coconut, tomato purée and curry sauce. Cook, stirring, until the coconut has dissolved. Reduce the heat to medium-low, cover and simmer for 5 mins.
4. Stir in the Quorn, cover and continue to simmer gently for 5 mins.
5. Slice the banana and add to the curry with the mango chutney. Season to taste and serve immediately.

CHEESY VEGETABLES
Serves two   *Takes approx. 15 mins.*

Lightly cooked vegetables in a creamy cheese sauce. Serve with a salad of sliced tomatoes and mild red onions sprinkled with oil and vinegar dressing, topped with a few black olives.

1 medium onion
4 young carrots
4 oz (100g) button mushrooms
8 oz (225g) broccoli
1 vegetable stock cube
½ pt (300ml) boiling water
2 slices bread
2 oz (50g) butter
1 tbsp (15ml) cornflour
¼ pt (150ml) whipping cream OR milk
3 tbsp (45ml) Parmesan cheese
Salt and freshly milled pepper

1. Peel and finely chop the onion. Scrub or peel the carrots and cut into very thin slices. Wipe and halve the mushrooms, if large. Cut the broccoli stems just below the sprouting 'head'. Break the 'head' into tiny sprigs (florets). Thinly slice the stems. Add the carrots and mushrooms to the broccoli and set aside.
2. Dissolve the stock cube into the boiling water.
3. Using a grater or processor, make the bread into crumbs, discarding the crusts. Melt half the butter in the frypan and stir in the crumbs. Cook, stirring, over medium-high heat until golden brown. Tip out onto paper towel.
4. Heat the remaining butter in the frypan and add the onion. Cook, stirring, over medium-high heat until just soft, about 2 mins. Add the other vegetables and the stock. Cover, reduce the heat to a gentle simmer and cook until the vegetables are just tender, about 4 mins.
5. Stir the cornflour thoroughly into the cream (or milk), add the cheese and seasoning. Gradually stir into the cooked vegetables and continue to cook, stirring constantly, until the sauce just comes to the boil and is thickened.
6. Spoon onto warm plates and sprinkle with the buttered crumbs. Serve immediately.

GREEN AND GOLD STIR FRY

Serves two   *Takes approx. 14 mins.*

Cashews are a favourite of mine to add rich flavour to stir fried vegetables, but almonds, pinenuts or roasted peanuts are very good too. When stir frying vegetables I prefer to choose just three or four kinds whose colours and shapes complement one another, rather than a haphazard larger selection.

Serve with hot herbed bread – this is simply French bread cut 'garlic-bread' style but spread with herbed, instead of garlic, butter before warming through.

2 tbsp (30ml) soy sauce
2 tbsp (30ml) dry sherry
2 tbsp (30ml) cold water
1 in (2.5cm) fresh ginger root
1 garlic clove
1 tbsp (15ml) cornflour
Salt and freshly milled pepper
6 oz (175g) young carrots
4 oz (100g) mangetout
6 spring onions
4 oz (100g) whole baby sweetcorn
1 tbsp (15ml) oil
4 oz (100g) cashew nuts

1. In a small bowl, combine the soy sauce, sherry and water. Peel and grate the ginger and add to the bowl. Peel and crush the garlic and add as well. Stir in the cornflour and salt and pepper to taste. Set aside.
2. Scrub or peel the carrots and cut into matchsticks. Top and tail the mangetout. Trim and cut the spring onions diagonally into 1 in/2.5cm pieces. Halve sweetcorn lengthwise if large. Set aside.
3. Heat the oil in the frypan, toss in the nuts and cook, stirring constantly, until golden brown. Remove with a slotted spoon onto paper towel.
4. Add the carrots and mangetout to the pan. Cook over high heat, stirring constantly, for 2 mins. Stir in the spring onions and sweetcorn and continue to cook, stirring, for 3 mins.

5. Stir the cornflour mixture thoroughly then pour it over the vegetables. Continue to cook, stirring constantly, until the sauce thickens and coats the vegetables.
6. Stir in the nuts and serve immediately.

8.   VEGETABLE FEASTS

BEANSPROUT SAUTÉ
Serves two   *Takes approx. 15 mins.*

This is a very crisp, healthy combination of fresh
vegetables and sprouted seeds dressed with a slightly
sweet soy and sherry glaze. I find it very useful to keep
cans of beansprouts in the cupboard but do use the fresh
variety if you prefer. You will find packs of ready-to-eat
mixed sprouted seeds in the refrigerated salad sections of
supermarkets and healthfood shops. Use any extra
sprouted seeds within twenty-four hours, I like them as a
sandwich filling or added to a mixed salad – they taste a
little like freshly picked raw peas! The courgettes and
carrots look very pretty cut into 'ribbons' with a swivel
potato peeler but if time is short, cut them diagonally into
paper-thin oval-shaped slices.
   Serve the Beansprout Sauté with warm granary rolls.

3 tbsp (45ml) soy sauce
2 tbsp (30ml) dry sherry
1 tbsp (15ml) cold water
1 tsp (5ml) clear honey
2 tsp (10ml) cornflour

(continued opposite)

(Beansprout Sauté continued)

Salt and freshly milled pepper
410g can beansprouts
6 oz (175g) young courgettes
6 oz (175g) young carrots
6 spring onions
1 tbsp (15ml) oil
4 oz (100g) mixed sprouted seeds
3 oz (75g) salted peanuts

1. Measure the soy sauce, sherry and water into a small bowl. Add the honey and whisk until dissolved. Sprinkle over the cornflour, salt and pepper to taste and whisk until smooth. Set aside.
2. Tip the canned beansprouts into a sieve and rinse under cold water. Leave in the sieve to drain.
3. Trim the courgettes and carrots and cut into thin strips with a swivel potato peeler or diagonally into paper-thin slices. Trim the spring onions and cut into 1 in/2.5cm pieces.
4. Heat the oil in the frypan. Add the courgettes, carrots and spring onions and cook over medium-high heat, stirring constantly, until they are soft – about 3 mins.
5. Add the beansprouts and mixed sprouted seeds. Cook, stirring constantly, for a minute or two.
6. Whisk the cornflour mixture (in case the cornflour has sunk to the bottom of the bowl) and pour it over the vegetables.
7. Continue to cook, stirring constantly, until the glaze has thickened and coated the vegetables.
8. Spoon onto hot plates and serve immediately, topped with the peanuts.

VEGETABLE CHOW-MEIN

Serves two　　　　　　　　　*Takes approx. 8 mins.*

The oriental food sections of most supermarkets have good selections of interesting vegetables such as bamboo shoots in small-sized cans, which are a useful stand-by in the cupboard. You will find egg noodles there too. They need very little cooking and make a simple stir fry of vegetables very filling. The Chow-mein goes well with a salad of finely sliced Chinese leaves and red pepper lightly tossed with an oil and vinegar dressing.

8 oz (225g) egg noodles
4 young carrots
2 oz (50g) young whole green beans
227g can bamboo shoots
2 tbsp (30ml) oil
1 tbsp (15ml) sesame seeds
4 tbsp (60ml) soy sauce

1. Cook the noodles according to package directions and leave to stand.
2. Peel or scrub the carrots and cut into matchsticks. Trim the beans and drain the bamboo shoots. Set aside.
3. Heat the oil in the frypan, toss in the sesame seeds and cook, stirring constantly, until beginning to brown.
4. Add the vegetables and cook, stirring, until just soft, about 2 mins.
5. Drain the noodles and add to the pan with the soy sauce. Mix well together and continue to cook, stirring, for 2 mins. longer. Serve immediately.

HOT POTATO SALAD

Serves two   *Takes approx. 10 mins.*

For the best result use new or salad potatoes in this recipe. They are available all the year round now and do not break up when cooked.

  Serve the Potato Salad freshly cooked with cold meats and crisp lettuce wedges.

4 celery sticks
1 clove garlic
4 spring onions
8 oz (225g) small new or salad potatoes
½ pt (300ml) cold water
2 tbsp + 1 tsp (30ml + 5ml) olive oil
1 tsp (5ml) whole-grain mustard
1 tsp (5ml) sugar
1 tsp (5ml) soy sauce
1 tbsp (15ml) red wine vinegar
Salt and freshly milled pepper

1. Thinly slice the celery, peel and crush the garlic. Trim and slice the spring onions diagonally. Set aside.
2. Scrub the potatoes, cutting into walnut-sized pieces if large. Add to the pan with the cold water, bring just to the boil, cover and gently cook until just soft, about 5 mins. Tip into a colander and leave to drain. Wipe the frypan with paper towel.
3. Thoroughly whisk together the 2 tbsp (30ml) oil, the mustard, sugar, soy sauce, vinegar and seasoning.
4. Heat the remaining oil in the frypan, add the celery and garlic and gently cook until just soft, about 2 mins.
5. Stir in the oil with the seasonings and bring just to the boil.
6. Remove from the heat, add the potatoes and spring onions and gently toss together. Serve immediately.

POTATO PANCAKE WITH SMOKED BACON

Serves two　　　　　　　　　　*Takes approx. 25 mins.*

The classic Swiss dish called Rösti is made with preboiled potatoes but that needs forward planning! I find I get an equally delicious result using uncooked grated potato plus a few extra ingredients. The recipe may look complicated but is actually quite simple. Crisp, smoked bacon rashers go well with the Pancake. Alternatively omit the bacon and sprinkle with grated mature Cheddar cheese after turning the pancake over.

Serve the Potato Pancake with a crunchy salad of crisp lettuce, thinly sliced celery and green apple slices topped with mayonnaise.

1 lb (450g) potatoes
1 medium onion
1 egg
2 tbsp (30ml) plain flour
1 tsp (5ml) baking powder
Salt and freshly milled pepper
4 rashers smoked back bacon
2 tbsp (30ml) oil

1. Peel the potatoes and coarsely grate, using a processor or cheese grater. Spread evenly over a clean tea-towel and roll up tightly Swiss-roll fashion. Twist the ends of the roll to extract excess moisture. Leave rolled up.
2. Grate the onion and put into a large bowl. Add the egg, flour and baking powder. Season to taste. Beat well to combine the ingredients thoroughly.
3. Cook the rashers of bacon in the frypan, over medium heat, until crisp and golden brown. Lift from the pan and keep hot. Remove the pan from the heat.
4. Tip all the grated potato into the onion and egg mixture. Beat well to combine evenly all the ingredients.
5. Heat 1 tbsp (15ml) oil in the frypan (do not wipe out after cooking the bacon). Add the potato mixture and cook over medium-high heat, stirring constantly, until

it begins to thicken.

6. Spread the potato mixture into an even layer and cover. Reduce the heat to medium-low and cook until the potatoes are soft in the centre and a rich golden brown underneath. (Don't break up the pancake, test the softness of the potatoes with a fork and just lift the edges of the pancake to check on the colour.)

7. Take the frypan off the heat. Place a baking tray or large plate on top of the frypan. Wearing oven gloves, reverse the pancake onto the baking tray.

8. Increase the heat to medium-high and heat the remaining oil in the pan. Slide in the potato pancake, brown side uppermost and continue to cook until golden brown on the base.

9. Cut the potato pancake in half and slide each portion onto a heated plate. Serve immediately topped with the bacon rashers.

CALIFORNIAN STIR FRY
Serves two   *Takes approx. 10 mins.*

The abundant variety of fruits and vegetables on the west coast of the United States inspires unexpected combinations of flavours. In this recipe quick cooking retains the bright green colour of the mangetout and broccoli, which look very pretty flecked with the orange peel – as well as tasting delicious too.

Serve with hot or cold roast chicken, or for a non-meat meal sprinkle with toasted nuts or sunflower seeds.

1 small orange
1 tbsp (15ml) clear honey
1 tbsp (15ml) white wine vinegar
1 tbsp (15ml) soy sauce
1 tsp (5ml) cornflour
4 oz (100g) mangetout
8 oz (225g) young broccoli
1 small onion

(continued overleaf)

(Californian Stir Fry continued)

1 in (2.5cm) fresh ginger root
1 clove garlic
1 tbsp (15ml) oil
Salt and freshly milled pepper

1. Coarsely grate the orange peel and set aside. Squeeze the juice into a measuring jug. If necessary make up to 3 fl oz (75ml) with water.
2. Add the honey, vinegar, soy sauce and cornflour to the juice. Whisk until smooth. Set aside.
3. Top and tail the mangetout. Remove the heads of the broccoli and break into tiny individual florets. Set aside. Trim off any leaves from the stems, and cut the stems into matchstick-sized pieces. Peel and finely slice the onion. Add the broccoli stems and the onion to the mangetout.
4. Peel and grate the ginger. Peel and crush the garlic.
5. Heat the oil in the frypan, stir in the grated orange peel, the ginger and the garlic. Cook over medium-high heat, stirring constantly, for 1 min.
6. Add the mangetout, the broccoli stems and the onion. Continue to cook, stirring constantly, for 3 mins.
7. Add the broccoli florets and cook, stirring, for 2 mins.
8. Stir the honey glaze, add to the pan and cook, stirring, for 1–2 mins. until the glaze has coated the vegetables. Season to taste. Serve immediately.

BOMBAY VEGETABLES
Serves two   *Takes approx. 15 mins.*

The last-minute addition of banana or mango to a lightly curry-spiced stir fry of vegetables adds a touch of unexpected sweetness, complemented by the cool, clean taste of the minted yoghurt sauce. Frying the spices with the onion for a few minutes really brings out all their warmth of flavour.

This recipe makes two generous servings. Serve with poppadums or warm Naan bread, adding rice for very hungry appetites.

4 tsp (20ml) mint jelly
6 tbsp (90ml) natural yoghurt
1 vegetable stock cube
½ pt (300ml) boiling water
6 oz (175g) young parsnips
6 oz (175g) young carrots
6 oz (175g) cauliflower florets
6 oz (175g) aubergine
1 small onion
2 cloves garlic
1 tbsp (15ml) oil
1 tsp (5ml) paprika
½ tsp (2.5ml) turmeric
½ tsp (2.5ml) ground cumin
½ tsp (2.5ml) ground coriander
½ tsp (2.5ml) chilli powder
1 tsp (5ml) sugar
2 medium firm bananas OR 1 mango
Salt and freshly milled pepper

1. Whisk the mint jelly into the yoghurt until smooth. Crumble the stock cube into the boiling water. Set both aside.
2. Peel or scrub the parsnips and carrots and cut into ½ in/1cm slices. Break the cauliflower into small pieces. Cut the aubergine into 1 in/2.5cm cubes, discarding the stem. Combine the vegetables and set aside.
3. Peel and thinly slice the onion. Peel and crush the garlic. Heat the oil in the frypan, stir in the onion and garlic and cook over medium-high heat, stirring, until soft.
4. Sprinkle over the spices and sugar. Continue to cook, stirring, for a minute or two.
5. Tip in the vegetables and stir to coat with the spice mixture. Add the stock, cover and reduce the heat to low. Simmer for 5 mins. or until the vegetables are just tender.
6. Peel and slice the bananas (or cube the mango) and gently stir into the vegetables. Cook for 1 min. Season to taste.
7. Serve immediately, spooning the minted yoghurt over the top.

PARSNIP AND PEPPER STIR FRY
Serves two   *Takes approx. 10 mins.*

A quick stir fry of slivers of young parsnips, sweet yellow pepper and spring onions in a sweet-sour glaze. Only use small parsnips as older vegetables may be tough and dry. Young carrots make a delicious alternative to parsnips.

Serve as a side dish with cold ham or grilled meats. To serve as a main dish, increase the bacon to 8 oz (225g).

8 oz (225g) young small parsnips
3 sticks celery
1 yellow pepper
6 spring onions
1 small lemon
2 tbsp (30ml) soy sauce
1 tbsp (15ml) white wine vinegar
2 tsp (10ml) tomato purée
1 tbsp (15ml) clear honey
1 tsp (5ml) cornflour
3 fl oz (75ml) cold water
2 oz (50g) streaky bacon
1 oz (25g) butter
Salt and pepper

1. Trim the stem end and root of the parsnips and peel. Cut into large matchstick slivers. Thinly slice the celery. Cut the pepper in half lengthwise, remove and discard the stem, seeds and pith. Cut into slivers. Add celery and pepper to the parsnips and set aside. Trim and slice the onions diagonally into 1 in/2.5cm pieces. Set aside.
2. Finely grate the lemon rind and squeeze the lemon for juice. Place the rind and juice into a small bowl and add the soy sauce, vinegar, tomato purée and honey. Sprinkle the cornflour over and whisk until smooth. Gradually whisk in the cold water.
3. Remove any bacon rinds and cut the bacon into small pieces. Cook in the frypan, stirring, over medium-high heat until crisp and brown. Remove from the pan with a slotted spoon.
4. Add the butter to the pan and stir in the parsnips,

celery and pepper. Cook, stirring constantly, until just soft. Add the onions and continue to cook for 1 min.
5. Stir the cornflour mixture and add to the frypan. Cook, stirring, until the glaze just comes to the boil, is smooth and slightly thickened.
6. Season to taste, stir in the bacon and serve immediately.

MUSHROOM FRICASSEE
Serves two   *Takes approx. 10 mins.*

Mushrooms in a rich creamy sauce make a very satisfying light meal.
Serve with rice, pasta or simply with crusty bread to mop up the delicious sauce. A quick salad of cherry tomatoes and diced cucumber tossed with oil and vinegar dressing goes well with the Fricassee.

1 small onion
4 celery sticks
12 oz (350g) button mushrooms
1 vegetable stock cube
3 fl oz (100ml) boiling water
2 fl oz (50ml) dry white vermouth
1 egg yolk
5 fl oz (150ml) sour cream
1 oz (25g) butter
2 oz (50g) fresh breadcrumbs
Freshly milled black pepper
2 tbsp (30ml) chopped parsley

1. Peel the onion and finely chop. Remove any celery leaves and keep for a garnish. Finely chop the sticks and add to the onion. Set aside.
2. Wipe the mushrooms with a dry cloth (there is no need to wash cultivated mushrooms) and trim the stems. Set aside.
3. Crumble the stock cube into a measuring jug and stir in the water. Add the vermouth.

4. In a small bowl, whisk the egg yolk into the sour cream.
5. Melt half the butter in the frypan, toss in the breadcrumbs and cook over high heat, stirring constantly, until golden brown. Tip onto paper towel.
6. Add the remaining butter to the pan with the onion and celery. Cook over medium heat, stirring, until soft. Stir in the mushrooms, increase the heat and continue to cook, stirring, until golden brown.
7. Pour in the stock/wine and cook, stirring, until the liquid has reduced to about half. Reduce the heat, stir in the egg yolk/sour cream and gently cook, stirring, until the sauce has thickened slightly.
8. Season to taste with pepper, stir in the parsley. Serve sprinkled with the crisp crumbs and garnished with the celery leaves.

MADISON AVENUE SPECIAL
Serves two　　　　　　　　　*Takes approx. 8 mins.*

I first ate this terrific salad in New York, hence the name, and it has been a special favourite of mine ever since. One thing is very important – you must use very well washed, very young tender spinach. Large tough leaves will ruin the salad. Look for the bags of ready-to-use tiny Italian spinach leaves which are perfect, in the ready-prepared vegetable section of supermarkets. Alternatively use finely sliced Chinese leaves or cos lettuce – quite different but also very good. Just serve hot rolls with this salad.

8 spring onions
1 ripe avocado
8 oz (225g) young spinach leaves
2 large slices fresh bread
4 oz (100g) smoked back bacon
2 tbsp (30ml) olive oil, preferably virgin
1 clove garlic
1 tbsp (15ml) red wine vinegar

(continued opposite)

(Madison Avenue Special continued)

1 tsp (5ml) whole-grain mustard
1 tsp (5ml) sugar
Salt and freshly milled pepper

1. Trim and diagonally slice the onions into 1 in/2.5cm pieces. Peel, stone and cut the avocado into large cubes. If necessary, wash and very thoroughly dry the spinach. Place onions, avocado and spinach leaves in a large bowl and set aside.
2. Cut the bread into small cubes, discarding the crusts if wished. Cut the bacon across into thin strips and place in the frypan. Cook, stirring, over medium heat until the fat has begun to run and the bacon starts to brown. Stir in the bread cubes and continue to cook, stirring constantly, until the bread is crisp and brown. Remove both bacon and bread from the pan with a slotted spoon and keep hot.
3. Add the oil to the pan. Peel and crush the garlic, add to the oil. Cook over medium-high heat until just soft.
4. Stir in the vinegar, mustard and sugar. Bring just to the boil. Season generously.
5. Immediately pour the dressing over the spinach, add the bacon and bread cubes and toss thoroughly together. Serve immediately and eat while the dressing, etc. is still hot.

WINTER STIR FRY
Serves two   *Takes approx. 10 mins.*

Crisply cooked vegetables in a richly flavoured glaze make a filling and inexpensive dish. Serve as the vegetable with meat or fish, or as the main dish with rice or noodles, completing the meal with cheese and biscuits.

Look for yellow bean paste in the oriental foods section of supermarkets. It adds flavour to all kinds of stir frys and should be kept in the fridge after opening. You will also find canned beansprouts in the same section. They are a

useful item to have in the cupboard when fresh beansprouts are not available.

4 small carrots
4 baby onions
6 oz (175g) wedge Savoy cabbage
3 celery sticks
4 oz (100g) beansprouts, fresh or canned
2 tbsp (30ml) sesame seeds
1 vegetable stock cube
½ pt (300ml) boiling water
2 tsp (10ml) cornflour
2 tbsp (30ml) soy sauce
3 tbsp (45ml) yellow bean paste
Salt and freshly milled pepper

1. Peel or scrub the carrots and cut into thin slices. Peel
    the onions and cut each into four wedges. Add to the
    carrots and set aside.
2. Remove any centre stem of the cabbage and very
    thinly slice cabbage into shreds. Thinly slice the celery
    and add to the cabbage. Drain the beansprouts if
    using canned. Set aside.
3. Sprinkle the sesame seeds in the frypan and cook over
    high heat, stirring constantly, until golden brown. Tip
    onto paper towel.
4. Dissolve the stock cube in the hot water. Pour about
    half into the frypan, add the carrots and onion
    wedges, cover and cook until almost tender, about 3
    mins.
5. Add the cabbage, celery and beansprouts to the pan
    and cook, stirring, until just beginning to soften.
    Remove from the heat.
6. Blend the cornflour to a cream with the soy sauce and
    add, with the bean paste, to the remaining stock.
7. Pour the stock over the vegetables, bring just to the
    boil and continue to cook, stirring constantly, until
    the glaze thickens and coats the vegetables. Stir in the
    sesame seeds and season to taste. Serve immediately.

CHINESE CHICKEN SALAD
Serves two   *Takes approx. 10 mins.*

The perfect dish for a summer lunch – tender slivers of spiced chicken with crunchy vegetables and a rich-flavoured dressing. Arrange the hot salad on a selection of fresh small-leaved salad greens such as Little Gem, Lamb's Lettuce and slightly peppery Rocket. If necessary, rinse the leaves under very cold water and dry very thoroughly in a tea-towel; wet salad leaves ruin a salad. Five spice powder is a Chinese blend of anise pepper, star anise, cassia or cinnamon, cloves and fennel which imparts a mild aniseed flavour. It is widely used in oriental dishes.

Serve with hot rolls followed by fresh berries and cream.

Selection of fresh salad leaves
1 bunch spring onions
227g can water chestnuts
2 boneless chicken breasts
1 tsp (5ml) five spice powder
1 oz (25g) pinenuts or flaked almonds
1 tbsp (15ml) mild-flavoured oil such as grapeseed
3 tbsp (45ml) soy sauce
Salt and freshly milled pepper

1. Arrange the salad leaves on two large plates.
2. Trim the spring onions and cut diagonally into 1 in/ 2.5cm pieces. Drain the water chestnuts and slice horizontally. Add to the spring onions and set aside.
3. Remove the chicken skin and cut the flesh into very thin strips. Sprinkle with the spice powder and, with your fingers, work it evenly into the chicken. Set aside.
4. Sprinkle the nuts in the frypan and cook, without any oil, over medium-high heat until golden brown. Stir frequently. Tip out onto a plate.
5. Heat the oil in the frypan and add the chicken pieces. Stir to separate. Cook, stirring frequently, over medium-high heat until crisp and brown. Remove from the pan with a slotted spoon and keep hot.

6. Add the spring onions and water chestnuts to the hot oil and cook, stirring, for 1 min. Sprinkle with the soy sauce, salt and pepper and bring just to the boil.
7. Remove the frypan from the heat and stir in the chicken. Spoon immediately over the salad greens and sprinkle with the nuts. Serve immediately.

9. FAST AND FILLING EGGS AND CHEESE

TUSCANY OMELETTE
Serves two   *Takes approx. 10 mins.*

The Italian answer to the Spanish omelette – or how to use up that left-over pasta! Just as the Spanish version uses a variety of previously cooked ingredients bound together with beaten egg so does the Italian. You need approximately 4 oz (100g) of cooked pasta, which weighs 2 oz (50g) before cooking. The other ingredients could be varied. Milano salami is seasoned with garlic and white wine. If unavailable, use bacon instead and cook it with the onion and pepper. Use another cooked vegetable such as green beans in place of the artichokes.

Serve with the coarse textured Italian bread made with olive oil that can now be found in most good stores. In Tuscany it would be served with a little dish of good quality olive oil to dip it into, instead of butter.

4 oz (100g) cooked pasta (see above)
1 small onion
2 cloves garlic

(continued overleaf)

(Tuscany Omelette continued)

1 red pepper
14 oz (397g) can artichoke halves
2 oz (50g) thinly sliced Italian salami
4 eggs
2 tbsp (30ml) cold water
Salt and freshly milled pepper
2 tbsp (30ml) olive oil
1 oz (25g) pitted green olives
1 oz (25g) grated Parmesan cheese

1. If necessary, cook the pasta and drain well.
2. Peel and finely chop the onion. Peel and crush the garlic. Halve the pepper lengthwise, discarding the stem, seeds and any pith. Cut into thin slices. Add garlic and pepper to the onion and set aside.
3. Drain the artichokes and halve if very large. Cut the salami into strips. Beat the eggs with the water and a *little* salt and pepper. Remember, the salami is a dried sausage and may be salty already. Set aside.
4. Heat the olive oil in the frypan and stir in the onion, garlic and pepper. Cook, stirring, over medium-high heat, until soft and beginning to brown.
5. Add the artichokes, salami, pasta and olives. Continue to cook, stirring, for 1 min.
6. Pour the eggs over and reduce the heat to medium. Cook, lifting the edges of the egg to allow uncooked egg to run underneath. Cook until all the egg is just set.
7. Sprinkle with the cheese and cut in half. Carefully slide each portion onto a warm plate and serve immediately.

EGGS AND PEPPERS WITH SMOKED BACON
Serves two   *Takes approx. 15 mins.*

This very simple recipe is based on a Portuguese dish where it is both cooked and served in the traditional heatproof brown pottery dishes. Do allow time for the peppers to get really soft before adding the eggs, using one or two per serving depending on your appetites! For a change use red and yellow peppers instead of green.

Serve the Eggs and Peppers in shallow pottery bowls with crusty bread. Add a salad of very thinly sliced red onions and ripe tomatoes, sprinkled with virgin olive oil, salt and pepper and whole black olives.

3 large green peppers
1 medium onion
4 rashers smoked streaky bacon
1 tbsp (15ml) olive oil
2 tsp (10ml) sugar
1 tbsp (15ml) red wine vinegar
Salt and freshly milled pepper
2–4 eggs

1. Halve the peppers, discarding the stems, seeds and any excess white pith. Cut into thin strips. Peel and thinly slice the onion.
2. Trim off any bacon rinds and cut the rashers into 1 in/ 2.5cm strips. Place in the frypan.
3. Cook over medium-high heat, stirring occasionally, until crisp and pale golden brown.
4. Add the oil, peppers and onions. Sprinkle with the sugar and vinegar and stir well. Reduce the heat to medium-low. Cover the pan and continue to cook until the peppers and onions are soft but not brown. Stir once or twice. This will take about 6–8 mins. Season to taste.
5. Make two (or four) shallow hollows in the peppers and break an egg into each. Cover the pan and cook, still over medium-low heat, until the eggs are just set. Serve immediately.

TAGLIATELLE WITH HERBED CHEESE

Serves two   *Takes approx. 8 mins.*

A carton of cream cheese flavoured with chives makes a
speedy sauce for pasta, with golden brown mushrooms
and smoked ham adding extra colour and flavour.

Add hot garlic rolls and a simple salad of wedges of
crisp lettuce sprinkled with oil and vinegar dressing to
complete the meal.

4 oz (100g) sliced smoked ham
6 oz (175g) tagliatelle
1 vegetable stock cube
4 fl oz (100ml) boiling water
4 oz (100g) button mushrooms
1 oz (25g) butter
125g carton cream cheese with chives
Salt and freshly milled pepper

1. Cut the slices of ham into thin ribbons. Set aside.
2. Cook the pasta according to package directions.
3. Crumble the stock cube into the water. Set aside.
4. Wipe the mushrooms with a soft cloth and trim the
    base of each. Cut into thin slices.
5. Heat the butter in the frypan and add the mushrooms.
    Cook over high heat, stirring constantly, until a rich
    golden brown.
6. Stir in the stock. Reduce the heat to medium and
    gradually blend in the cream cheese, stirring to
    combine with the stock.
7. Heat gently until just bubbling. Season to taste then
    remove from the heat.
8. Drain the pasta and add to the pan. Lightly toss
    together then divide between two hot plates.
9. Top with the finely shredded ham and serve immedi-
    ately.

BACON AND EGG WITH A DIFFERENCE
Serves two   *Takes approx. 10 mins.*

A fresh twist to our favourite breakfast foods! Serve piping hot at any time of the day for a very satisfying meal.

1 egg
¼ pt (150ml) milk
Salt and freshly milled pepper
1 tsp (5ml) whole-grain mustard
2 large thick slices fresh bread
4 rashers back bacon
1 large eating apple
1 oz (25g) butter

1. Break the egg into a medium bowl and add the milk, salt, pepper and mustard. Whisk until thoroughly combined.
2. Carefully pour onto a large plate.
3. Trim the crusts from the bread if wished and cut each slice in half.
4. Slide each piece of bread into the egg mixture, turning (easiest using two forks) to coat on both sides. Leave all four pieces of bread on the plate to absorb all the egg mixture.
5. Place the bacon rashers in the frypan and cook over medium-high heat until crisp and golden brown.
6. While the bacon is cooking peel and core the apple and cut across into four slices.
7. Remove the bacon from the pan and keep hot.
8. Melt half the butter in the pan and add the apple slices. Cook, turning carefully, until golden brown on both sides.
9. Remove from the pan and keep hot with the bacon.
10. Heat the remaining butter in the pan and carefully add the pieces of soaked bread. Cook, turning carefully, until golden brown on both sides.
11. Place two pieces of the bread on each serving plate and top with the bacon and apple slices. Serve immediately.

SWISS CORN AND POTATO BAKE

Serves two   *Takes approx. 18 mins.*

Cheese, eggs, corn and potatoes make an extremely tasty combination in this very quick and filling meal. Use one or two eggs per serving depending on your appetites. I like to use the Swiss Gruyère cheese in this recipe but any firm cheese that will grate will be equally successful.

Serve with a simple salad of wedges of cos lettuce topped with a spoonful of mayonnaise and sprinkled with chives.

4 oz (100g) Gruyère cheese
7 oz (198g) can sweetcorn
12 oz (350g) potatoes
1 medium onion
1 tbsp (15ml) olive oil
Salt and freshly milled pepper
2–4 eggs

1. Grate the cheese and set aside. Tip the corn into a sieve and leave to drain.
2. Peel or scrub the potatoes and cut into ½ in/1cm cubes. Peel and thinly chop the onion.
3. Heat the oil in the frypan and add the onion. Cook over medium heat, stirring, until soft but not brown.
4. Add the potatoes and mix well. Reduce the heat to medium-low, cover the pan and cook until the potatoes are soft, stirring once or twice. This will take 6–8 mins.
5. When the potatoes are soft (test with the point of a knife) increase the heat to medium-high and add the corn. Continue to cook, uncovered and stirring constantly, until the potatoes are golden brown.
6. Make two (or four) hollows in the potatoes and break an egg into each. Season to taste and sprinkle with the grated cheese.
7. Cover the frypan and cook for a further 2–3 mins. or until the eggs are just set and the cheese melted. Serve immediately.

SPINACH AND BACON FRITTATA

Serves two   *Takes approx. 15 mins.*

A very light, fresh-tasting dish – just right for lunch or a late supper. Don't be dismayed by the seemingly large amount of spinach – it will very quickly cook down. Thawed, frozen leaf spinach can be used but the end result won't be quite so delicious. Do use wine vinegar for cooking – keep the malt just for the fish and chips!

Very good with a salad of sliced ripe tomatoes just sprinkled with a little sugar, salt and pepper. Plus lots of crusty bread.

8 oz (225g) fresh young spinach
3 eggs
4 oz (100g) smoked streaky bacon
1 small onion
1 tsp (5ml) oil
2 tsp (10ml) red wine vinegar
Salt and freshly milled pepper
2 oz (50g) Cheddar cheese, grated

1. Tear off any thick stems and very thoroughly wash the spinach in several changes of cold water. It is often very sandy and if it's not all removed, will make a gritty Frittata. Drain well, spread over a tea-towel and roll up tightly to remove the water. Tip onto a cutting board, roll up into a rough ball and cut across into 2 in/5cm ribbons. Set aside.
2. Whisk the eggs with a fork and set aside.
3. Remove any rinds from the bacon and cut across into 1 in/2.5cm pieces. Peel and finely chop the onion.
4. Heat the oil in the frypan and stir in the bacon and onion. Cook, stirring, over medium heat, until the bacon is beginning to brown and the onion is soft.
5. Gradually add the spinach. It will cook down very quickly. Sprinkle the vinegar and seasoning over. Cover and cook for a few minutes, until the spinach is quite soft.
6. Pour the beaten eggs over and continue to cook over medium heat, lifting the edge of the Frittata to allow uncooked egg to run underneath.

7. Sprinkle the cheese over, replace the lid and cook for 1 min. to allow the cheese to melt. Cut in half and gently slide each onto hot plates. Serve immediately.

PIPERADE
Serves two   *Takes approx. 25 mins.*

Piperade is a simple dish of creamy scrambled eggs, onions and sweet peppers from the Basque region of France. Allow enough time for the vegetables to cook slowly for the best flavour. Many shops sell packs of mixed fresh herbs such as basil, marjoram and chives. Keep in the fridge and use in salads or add to freshly cooked rice or pasta for a very fresh herb flavour. If not available, use the freeze-dried variety.

I like to serve Piperade with slices of cold smoked ham and hot buttered toast.

3 eggs
2 tbsp (30ml) milk
Salt and freshly milled pepper
1 large onion (about 4 oz (100g))
1 large red pepper
6 oz (175g) ripe tomatoes (OR 1 large beefsteak tomato)
1 tbsp (15ml) olive oil
1 tsp (5ml) sugar
1 tbsp (15ml) chopped fresh mixed herbs

1. Break the eggs into a medium bowl and add the milk and seasoning. Whisk until well combined. Set aside.
2. Peel and very thinly slice the onion. Halve the pepper lengthwise, discarding the seeds and stem. Cut the flesh into thin slices. Halve the tomatoes discarding the tough base of the stem. Cut into small wedges.
3. Heat the oil in the frypan over medium-low heat. Stir in the onion slices and sprinkle with the sugar. Stirring occasionally, let the onion cook slowly until soft and a pale gold, about 5 mins.
4. Add the pepper slices and continue to cook slowly

until soft, about another 5 mins.

5. Add the tomatoes, cover and continue to cook for a further 5 mins. or until the vegetables are very soft.
6. Pour the beaten eggs over and sprinkle with the herbs.
7. Continue to cook over medium-low heat, gently pushing the cooked egg to the centre of the pan until it is all just set but still very creamy.
8. Spoon onto hot serving plates and serve immediately.

SPICY SAUSAGE SCRAMBLE
Serves two   *Takes approx. 8 mins.*

The fiery little red or green chilli peppers used extensively in South American dishes and Indian curries, are now widely available in our stores. Treat them with respect, a little goes a long way, and always wash your hands well after handling them as they may make your skin tingle. In this simple recipe just a little chopped fresh chilli pepper adds extra zip to scrambled eggs with sausages. If you have none handy add a dash of bottled chilli or hot pepper sauce.

Serve the Spicy Sausage Scramble with hot crusty rolls or toast.

3 eggs
2 tbsp (30ml) cold water
Salt and freshly milled pepper
4 pork sausages
1 small onion
1 small fresh chilli
1 tsp (5ml) oil

1. Break the eggs into a medium bowl and add the water and seasoning to taste. Whisk until thoroughly combined. Set aside.
2. Slit the sausage skins and peel off. Break the sausage meat into small pieces with a fork.
3. Peel and finely chop the onion. Split the chilli,

removing and discarding the seeds and stem. Very finely chop the flesh and add to the onion.

4. Heat the oil in the frypan and stir in the onion and chilli. Cook, stirring constantly, over medium heat until soft.
5. Add the sausage meat and continue to cook, stirring, until the meat is golden brown. Carefully pour off any excess fat.
6. Pour the beaten eggs over and cook, stirring constantly, until they are just set and still creamy in consistency. (Scrambled eggs are best when cooked until just set, not until they are firm and dry.)
7. Spoon onto hot plates and serve immediately.

ASPARAGUS OMELETTE
Serves two   *Takes approx. 8 mins.*

The first tender crop of asparagus in the spring deserves very simple yet special cooking. Here I have just very lightly stir fried it with a few spring onions and then added beaten eggs to make a flat omelette. I agree the addition of a little cream on top is indulgent but it does make a delicious finish to a very pretty dish.

Serve as a light lunch or supper with warm rolls, crisp celery sticks and some Cheshire cheese.

4 eggs
2 tbsp (30ml) cold water
Salt and freshly milled pepper
4 spring onions
8 oz (225g) young asparagus
1 oz (25g) butter
3 tbsp (45ml) double cream

1. Break the eggs into a medium-sized bowl, add the water and seasoning to taste. Whisk with a fork to blend together thoroughly. Set aside.
2. Trim the spring onions and cut into 1 in/2.5cm pieces.
3. Cut the asparagus stalks diagonally 2 in/5cm from the

tip. Set tips aside. Trim off any woody end and discard. Cut the remaining stalks diagonally into 2 in/ 5cm pieces. Add to the spring onions.

4. Heat the butter in the frypan and add the spring onions and asparagus stalks. Cook over medium-high heat, stirring constantly until the asparagus is just beginning to feel soft when pierced with the tip of a knife – about 3 mins.

5. Add the asparagus tips and continue to cook for 1 min. longer.

6. Pour the beaten eggs over and continue to cook, lifting the edges of the omelette as they set, allowing the uncooked egg to run underneath them.

7. When all the egg is set and the omelette is a pale golden brown on the underneath (don't try to turn or fold this omelette, just lift the edges with a flat knife to check whether it is brown enough), drizzle the cream over. Remove the pan from the heat, cover and leave to stand for 1 min.

8. Cut the omelette in half and gently slide each portion onto warm plates. Serve immediately.

HOT CHEESE SANDWICHES

Hot Cheese Sandwiches have a crunchy golden brown exterior with a delicious melting savoury filling – far more appetising than a straight cheese sandwich but using no more effort! These are my four favourite fillings but I am sure you can think up many more.

Very good just on their own or you can add a carton of coleslaw salad, a packet of crisps and a piece of fresh fruit to make a quick meal.

Each variation serves two and takes approx. 6 mins.

Italian style
    4 slices thinly cut fresh bread
    soft butter
    1.76 oz (50g) can anchovies in olive oil
    5 oz (150g) Mozzarella cheese
    1 oz (25g) black olives (optional)

1. Cut off the crusts of the bread and lightly spread with soft butter.
2. Drain the anchovies, reserving the oil. Coarsely chop the fish and spread evenly over two of the slices of bread.
3. Thinly slice the cheese and arrange on top of the anchovies.
4. Top with the remaining two slices of bread and press lightly together. Cut each sandwich in half.
5. Heat the reserved olive oil in the frypan and add the sandwiches. Cook over medium-high heat until golden brown on both sides, turning carefully with a spatula.
6. Place a paper napkin on two serving plates and top each with two sandwiches. Serve immediately, garnished with olives if wished.

Nutty Goat's Cheese
   4 slices thinly-cut fresh granary bread
   soft butter
   3 oz (75g) walnuts
   6 oz (175g) Chèvre (goat's) cheese
   Pickled walnuts (optional)

1. Cut off the crusts of the bread and lightly spread with butter.
2. Roughly chop the walnuts and sprinkle over two of the slices of bread.
3. Cut the cheese into thin slices (no need to remove the rind) and arrange on top of the nuts.
4. Top with the remaining two slices of bread and press lightly together. Cut each sandwich in half.
5. Heat a knob of butter in the frypan and add the sandwiches.
6. Cook over medium-high heat until golden brown on both sides, turning carefully with a spatula.
7. Place a paper napkin on two serving plates and top each with two sandwiches. Serve immediately, garnished with pickled walnuts if wished.

Traditional English
4 slices thinly-cut fresh wholemeal bread
soft butter
English mustard
4 small sticks celery
4 oz (100g) Stilton cheese
Celery leaves to garnish

1. Cut off the crusts of the bread and lightly spread with butter and a little mustard.
2. Finely chop the celery and sprinkle over two slices of bread.
3. Crumble the Stilton with a fork and arrange over the top of the celery.
4. Top with the remaining slices of bread and lightly press together. Cut each sandwich in half.
5. Heat a knob of butter in the frypan and add the sandwiches.
6. Cook over medium-high heat until golden brown on both sides, turning carefully with a spatula.
7. Place a paper napkin on two serving plates and top each with two sandwiches. Serve immediately, garnished with the celery leaves.

Ham and Pickled Cheese
4 slices thinly-cut mixed grains bread
soft butter
2 thin slices ham
4 oz (100g) Cheddar cheese
4 tbsp (60ml) sweet brown pickle
pickled onions (optional)

1. Cut off the crusts of the bread and thinly spread with butter.
2. Top two slices with the ham.
3. Grate the Cheddar cheese and blend with the pickle. Evenly spread over the ham.
4. Top with the remaining slices of bread and lightly press together. Cut each sandwich in half.
5. Heat a knob of butter in the frypan and add the sandwiches.

6. Cook over medium-high heat until golden brown on both sides, turning carefully with a spatula.
7. Place a paper napkin on two serving plates and top each with two sandwiches. Serve immediately, garnished with pickled onions if wished.

10. PASTA PERFECT

TAHINI AND SAUSAGE SPAGHETTI SAUCE
Serves two   *Takes approx. 10 mins.*

A new twist to spaghetti and meatballs – tiny sausage meatballs in a sesame-flavoured sauce made with tahini paste. The amount of pasta depends on your appetite!

Serve the pasta and sauce with a glowing salad of grated carrot, sultanas and fresh orange segments tossed with a dressing made of olive oil and lemon juice.

8–12 oz (225–350g) spaghetti
1 vegetable stock cube
½ pt (300ml) boiling water
1 lemon
4 tbsp (60ml) tahini paste
3 tbsp (45ml) soy sauce
2 tbsp (30ml) clear honey
Salt and freshly milled pepper
1 clove garlic
1 tbsp (15ml) flour
1 tsp (5ml) freeze-dried mixed herbs
8 oz (225g) sausagemeat
1 tbsp (15ml) oil

1. Cook the spaghetti according to package directions.
2. Crumble the stock cube into the water in a medium bowl. Squeeze the juice from the lemon and add to the bowl with the tahini paste, soy sauce, honey, salt and pepper. Whisk together until smooth. Set aside.
3. Peel and crush the garlic. Set aside.
4. Spoon the flour onto a sheet of greaseproof paper and add the herbs. Season with salt and pepper and mix well together.
5. Divide the sausagemeat into twelve pieces and shape into balls with your fingers. Add to the seasoned flour and toss to coat thoroughly.
6. Heat the oil in the frypan and add the sausagemeat balls. Shaking the pan frequently, cook over medium-high heat until golden brown on all sides. Remove from the pan with a slotted spoon.
7. Add the garlic to the pan and cook, stirring, for 30 seconds.
8. Off the heat pour the tahini mixture into the pan. Lower heat to medium and bring the sauce just to the boil, stirring constantly.
9. Return the sausagemeat balls to the pan, cover and simmer for 5 mins., stirring once or twice.
10. Drain the pasta, pile into warm bowls and spoon the sausagemeat balls and sauce over the top. Serve immediately.

SPAGHETTI WITH BROCCOLI AND SMOKED CHEESE

Serves two   *Takes approx. 15 mins.*

Smoked cheese has a very subtle flavour which combines well with fresh broccoli. The degree of 'smokiness' varies with the country of origin and the type of cheese smoked. I particularly like a British cheese defined as 'applewood smoked'.

Warm granary bread and a salad of sliced apples, celery and walnuts would go well with this dish.

4 oz (100g) spaghetti
4 oz (100g) smoked cheese
1 vegetable stock cube
½ pt (300ml) boiling water
12 oz (350g) young broccoli
1 tbsp (15ml) olive oil
Salt and freshly milled pepper

1. Cook the spaghetti according to package directions.
2. Grate or dice the cheese, depending on how soft a cheese it is. Crumble the stock cube into the boiling water. Set aside.
3. Cut off the heads of the broccoli and break into individual tiny florets. Trim the ends of the stems then cut into very thin slices.
4. Heat the oil in the frypan and add the sliced broccoli stems. Cook, stirring, over medium-high heat for 3–4 mins.
5. Add the florets and stir to coat with the oil.
6. Pour the stock over and bring just to the boil.
7. Continue to cook, stirring, until the stock has reduced to just a few spoonfuls and the broccoli is tender – 3–4 mins. Remove from the heat and season to taste.
8. Drain the pasta and divide between two warm bowls. Spoon the sauce over and top with the cheese. Serve immediately.

PASTA QUILLS WITH ASPARAGUS AND HAM

Serves two   *Takes approx. 15 mins.*

Tender stalks of young asparagus combined with pasta of a similar shape, plus slivers of smoked ham are a delight to the eye and delicious to eat. Light cooking enhances the beautiful emerald green colour of the asparagus and the hazelnut oil adds a very subtle final touch.

Serve with warm crusty bread and a sliced tomato salad.

4 oz (100g) pasta quills (penne)
12 oz (350g) young asparagus
4 oz (100g) sliced smoked ham
1 oz (25g) hazelnuts
½ oz (15g) butter
5 fl oz (150ml) cold water
1 vegetable stock cube
2 tbsp (30ml) hazelnut oil

1. Cook the pasta according to package directions.
2. Cut the asparagus stalks diagonally 2 in/5cm from the tip. Set aside. Trim off the woody ends and discard. Cut remaining stalks into 2 in/5cm lengths diagonally. Slice the ham into thin ribbons.
3. Roughly chop the hazelnuts. Melt the butter in the fry-pan, stir in the nuts and cook, stirring constantly, over medium heat until golden brown. Tip out onto paper towel. Carefully wipe out the pan with paper towel.
4. Add the water to the pan, crumble over the stock cube and bring to the boil, stirring.
5. Toss in the asparagus stems (not the tips) and cook over high heat, for about 3 mins., stirring constantly. Add the asparagus tips and continue to cook, gently tossing the vegetables, until they are just tender. Be careful not to overcook; they should still be slightly crisp. Stir in the ham. Remove from the heat.
6. Thoroughly drain the pasta and gently add to the pan, with the hazelnuts. Dribble the hazelnut oil over and serve immediately.

VEGETABLE PASTA WITH GARLIC CROÛTONS

Serves two   *Takes approx. 12 mins.*

A carton of garlic- and herb-flavoured cream cheese makes a quick creamy sauce for freshly cooked pasta and mixed vegetables. Try other flavoured cream cheeses and different vegetables to vary the dish.

Serve in shallow bowls with crusty bread.

1 large slice of bread
1 clove garlic
1 oz (25g) butter
6 oz (175g) pasta shells
1 medium onion
1 tbsp (15ml) olive oil
1 vegetable stock cube
3 fl oz (75ml) boiling water
8 oz (225g) frozen mixed vegetables
5 oz (150g) carton full-fat soft cheese with garlic and herbs

1. Cut the slice of bread into ½ in/1cm cubes (trim off the crust first, if wished). Peel and crush the garlic.
2. Heat the butter in the frypan, toss in the bread cubes and garlic. Cook, stirring constantly, over high heat until golden brown. Tip out onto paper towel. Set aside.
3. Cook the pasta according to package directions.
4. Peel and finely chop the onion. Heat the oil in the frypan. Stir in the onion and cook, stirring, over medium heat until soft.
5. Dissolve the stock cube in the water, add to the pan with the frozen vegetables. Cover and cook, over medium-high heat, until the vegetables are very hot.
6. Gradually add the cheese, stirring over medium heat until melted.
7. Thoroughly drain the pasta, stir into the vegetables and cook a minute or two longer. Spoon into hot bowls and sprinkle with the croûtons.

LEEK AND TUNA CHEESE
Serves two   *Takes approx. 12 mins.*

My variation of an old favourite. Using a mature Cheddar gives the strength of flavour needed yet uses less cheese than would be required with milder cheese. The tuna is optional. A tasty variation is to use some sliced, cooked sausages or 4 oz (100g) diced corned beef instead. If you haven't any dry mustard powder, add a tiny pinch of nutmeg.

This makes two generous portions. Serve with a quick salad of tomato wedges and diced cucumber tossed with lemon juice, olive oil and seasoning.

4 oz (100g) macaroni
8 oz (225g) young leeks
6 oz (175g) mature Cheddar
3½ oz (80g) can tuna in brine
2 large slices fresh bread
1½ oz (40g) butter
1 tbsp (15ml) flour
Pinch dry mustard
¾ pt (400ml) milk

1. Cook the macaroni according to package directions. Drain well.
2. Clean and thinly slice the leeks. Grate the cheese. Drain and flake the tuna. Set aside.
3. Make the bread into crumbs, discarding the crusts. Melt ½ oz (15g) of the butter in the frypan and stir in the crumbs. Cook, stirring, over medium-high heat, until golden brown. Remove from the pan.
4. Melt the remaining butter in the frypan and add the leeks. Cover and cook over medium heat until very soft, stirring once or twice, about 5 mins.
5. Stir in the flour and mustard. Cook, stirring, for 1 min. Gradually blend in the milk. Bring to the boil, stirring constantly, and cook until smooth and thickened.
6. Add the cheese and continue to cook, stirring, until melted.
7. Gently fold in the pasta and flaked tuna.
8. Spoon onto hot plates and sprinkle with the crisp crumbs. Serve immediately.

SALMON TETRAZZINNI
Serves two   *Takes approx. 10 mins.*

This is another recipe collected on my trips to the USA though there you are more likely to find it with canned tuna. I think it is equally good with either fish, so please try both.

A simple salad of crisp lettuce and cherry tomatoes tossed with oil and vinegar dressing goes very nicely with Salmon Tetrazzinni.

6 oz (150g) pasta shapes
4 oz (100g) button mushrooms
4 oz (100g) Cheddar cheese
7.5 oz (212g) can salmon, pink or red
1 small onion
1 oz (25g) flaked almonds
1 oz (25g) butter
1 tbsp (15ml) flour
8 fl oz (225ml) milk
2 fl oz (50ml) dry white vermouth
Salt and freshly milled pepper

1. Cook the pasta according to package directions.
2. Wipe and slice the mushrooms. Grate the cheese. Drain the salmon and break into large pieces, discarding skin and bones. Peel and finely chop the onion. Set aside.
3. Sprinkle the almonds into the frypan and cook, stirring constantly, over medium-high heat, until golden brown. Tip the nuts onto paper towel.
4. Melt the butter in the frypan and stir in the mushrooms and onion. Cook, stirring, over medium-high heat, until golden brown. Remove the pan from the heat.
5. Sprinkle the flour over and stir into the vegetables. Gradually stir in the milk and the vermouth.
6. Cook, stirring constantly, over medium heat until the sauce comes to the boil and is smooth and slightly thickened. Sprinkle the cheese over and stir until melted. Season to taste.
7. Thoroughly drain the pasta and add to the pan, with the salmon. Gently blend into the sauce.
8. Serve immediately, sprinkled with the almonds.

FRESH SPINACH AND CHEESE SAUCE WITH FUSILLI

Serves two   *Takes approx. 18 mins.*

Finely shredded fresh spinach, lightly cooked then combined with fromage frais makes a very pretty sauce for
pasta. Fromage frais – literally 'fresh cheese' – has a very
clean light taste. I prefer to use the slightly richer 8%
version in this recipe (it has a little cream added to it) but
the 1% version may also be used. Pimentos are a variety
of Spanish sweet red pepper sold packed in olive oil in
cans. They add a vivid touch of colour to the green and
white sauce. Empty any unused pimentos out of the tin
into a covered container and store in the refrigerator. Use
in a salad or add to cooked rice. I choose the pasta called
fusilli – the shape that looks like a corkscrew – to serve
with this sauce.

   Serve with a salad of sliced ripe tomatoes and radishes
sprinkled with coarse sea salt and freshly milled pepper.
Add some crisp Italian breadsticks too.

8 oz (225g) fusilli pasta shapes
8 oz (225g) young fresh spinach
2 canned pimentos
1 oz (25g) flaked almonds
1 medium onion
2 cloves garlic
1 tbsp (15ml) olive oil
1 tbsp (15ml) flour
½ tsp (2.5ml) ground nutmeg
¼ pt (150ml) milk
4 oz (100g) 8% fromage frais
Grated Parmesan cheese
Salt and freshly milled pepper

1. Cook the pasta according to package directions.
2. Very thoroughly wash the spinach in cold running
    water to remove every particle of sand that may be in
    it. Drain then lay out on a clean towel. Roll up like a
    swiss-roll to squeeze out all the water clinging to it.
    Remove from the towel and very finely shred. Set
    aside.

3. Drain the pimentos on paper towel then cut into thin strips. Set aside.
4. Tip the almonds into the frypan and cook over medium-high heat until golden brown, stirring constantly. Tip onto paper towel and set aside.
5. Peel and finely chop the onion. Peel and crush the garlic. Heat the oil in the frypan, add the onion and garlic and cook over medium-high heat until just soft and golden brown, stirring frequently.
6. Add the spinach and continue to cook, stirring once or twice, until soft – about 3 mins.
7. Remove from the heat and sprinkle the flour and nutmeg over. Return to the heat and cook for 1 min.
8. Gradually stir in the milk and cook until the sauce is smooth and thickened, stirring constantly.
9. Reduce the heat to medium-low and blend in the fromage frais and pimento strips. Continue to simmer gently until heated through. Season to taste.
10. Drain the pasta and add to the sauce, lightly blending together.
11. Divide betwen two warm bowls and top with the almonds. Serve immediately with the Parmesan cheese sprinkled on top.

SEAFOOD TAGLIATELLE
Serves two   *Takes approx. 14 mins.*

A very special dish for a special meal. Fresh scallops are in season from October to March but are available frozen all the year round. When bought fresh they should still have the orange roe (called the coral) attached. Include these in the recipe. Rinse fresh scallops in cold water before use to remove all traces of sand, or defrost the frozen variety. The softened cucumber garnish looks very pretty lightly piled on the top of each serving.

Serve the Seafood Tagliatelle with a salad of pink and white grapefruit segments, very finely sliced sweet red onion and watercress sprigs sprinkled with oil and vinegar dressing.

8–12 oz (225–350g) tagliatelle verdi (green pasta noodles)
8 oz (225g) scallops
4 in (10cm) piece cucumber
Boiling water
1 medium onion
2 small carrots
1 clove garlic
1 tbsp (15ml) olive oil
1 tbsp (15ml) flour
½ tsp (2.5ml) ground coriander
2 fl oz (50ml) dry white vermouth
¼ pt (150ml) double cream
1 tbsp (15ml) chopped chives or parsley

1. Cook the tagliatelle according to package directions.
2. Cut the scallops across into thick slices if large (leave the coral, if any, whole). Set aside.
3. Halve the cucumber and scoop out the seeds. Cut the flesh into matchstick-sized pieces, place in a small bowl and cover with boiling water. Set aside.
4. Peel and finely chop the onion. Scrub or peel the carrots and cut into matchstick-sized pieces. Peel and crush the garlic.
5. Heat the oil in the frypan and stir in the vegetables. Cook over medium heat until soft and the onion is pale golden brown, stirring constantly.
6. Sprinkle the flour and coriander over and cook for 1 min., stirring constantly.
7. Remove the pan from the heat and add the vermouth and the cream.
8. Reduce the heat to medium. Stirring constantly, bring the sauce just to the boil.
9. Stir in the scallops (reserve any corals). Cover and gently simmer for 5 mins., adding the corals, if any, for the last minute. Season to taste.
10. Thorougly drain the pasta and pile into warm bowls.
11. Thoroughly drain the cucumber and lightly mix with the chives (or parsley).
12. Spoon the scallops and sauce over the pasta and top with the wilted cucumber/chives (or parsley) garnish. Serve immediately.

SMOKED FISH WITH PASTA SHELLS
Serves two   *Takes approx. 12 mins.*

A piquant sauce of yoghurt and mayonnaise goes well with the slightly smoky taste of the fish. Not only are the pasta shells appropriately shaped for a fish dish, they also fill with tiny pools of the sauce.

Serve the pasta dish with a crisp salad of cos lettuce and finely sliced celery tossed with a lemony oil and vinegar dressing.

6 oz (175g) pasta shells
5 fl oz (150ml) natural yoghurt
2 tbsp (30ml) mayonnaise
1 tsp (5ml) cornflour
1 vegetable stock cube
¼ pt (150ml) boiling water
Half a lemon
8 oz (225g) smoked fish – cod or haddock
4 oz (100g) shelled prawns OR 200g can
6 spring onions
1 oz (25g) butter
Salt and freshly milled pepper
Grated Parmesan cheese

1. Cook the pasta shells according to package directions.
2. Whisk together the yoghurt, mayonnaise and cornflour. Crumble the stock cube into the water. Squeeze the lemon for juice and add to the stock. Set aside.
3. Remove any skin and bones from the fish and cut into bite-sized pieces. If using canned prawns, drain them.
4. Trim the spring onions and cut into 1 in/2.5cm pieces.
5. Heat the butter in the frypan and add the onions and smoked fish. Cook over medium-high heat, stirring constantly, until the fish looks opaque. Stir carefully to avoid breaking up the pieces of fish.
6. Add the stock and prawns. Reduce the heat to medium-low and gently simmer for 5 mins.
7. Stir in the yoghurt sauce and heat through until bubbling hot. Season to taste.
8. Drain the pasta and divide between two warm bowls. Spoon the sauce over and serve immediately with the cheese ready to sprinkle on top.

PIZZA PASTA
Serves two   *Takes approx. 10 mins.*

Simply take the favourite toppings of pizza – tomatoes, onions, olives and anchovies and make a quick sauce for pasta. I like to use the pasta shape called Orecchiette as this combines visually with the round tomatoes and olives. The name comes from the Italian word for ear – orecchio, and this is exactly what the little shapes look like. You should be able to find Orecchiette in Italian delicatessens but if not, use small shell pasta.

Serve this substantial dish with a salad of chunky pieces of iceberg lettuce and diced green skinned eating apples, topped with mayonnaise and broken walnuts.

6 oz (175g) Orecchiette pasta
1 large onion
2 cloves garlic
8 oz (225g) cherry tomatoes
2 slices fresh bread
1.76 oz (50g) can anchovies
2 tbsp (30ml) virgin olive oil
1 vegetable stock cube
¼ pt (150ml) boiling water
1 tbsp (15ml) red wine vinegar
2 oz (50g) black olives
Freshly milled pepper

1.   Cook the pasta according to package directions.
2.   Peel and thinly slice the onion. Peel and crush the garlic and add to the onion. Set aside. Remove any stems from the tomatoes, rinse and dry.
3.   Remove the crusts from the bread and make into crumbs (in a food processor or with a grater). Drain the oil from the anchovies into the frypan. Cut into half and separate all the little anchovies.
4.   Add the crumbs and anchovies to the anchovy oil and cook, over medium heat, stirring constantly, until crisp and golden brown. Remove from the pan.
5.   Pour the olive oil into the frypan, stir in the onion and garlic. Cook over medium heat, stirring, until soft and golden brown. Stir in the whole tomatoes.

6. Crumble the stock cube over and stir in the water and vinegar. Gently cook for a minute or two just to soften the tomatoes. Try not to break them.
7. Stir in the olives, season to taste. Well drain the pasta and add to the pan.
8. Spoon onto hot plates or bowls and top with the anchovy crumbs. Serve immediately.

11.   RICE IS NICE

JAMBALAYA
Serves two   *Takes approx. 20 mins.*

Creole cookery, from New Orleans in the south of the
USA, is a wonderful blend of French, Spanish and Indian
cooking, reflecting the influences of the people who, for
various reasons, settled there. Using local ingredients, the
recipes reflect the Creole ability to produce rich yet subtle
dishes from relatively inexpensive ingredients. Jambalaya
is just that – the Creole way of combining small amounts
of meat, fish and vegetables not unlike the Spanish paella.

Serve Jambalaya with very hot Garlic Toasts – slices of
French bread drizzled with virgin olive oil, sprinkled with
crushed garlic and grilled until golden brown.

1 large onion
2 cloves garlic
1 large green pepper
1 chicken stock cube
½ pt (300ml) boiling water
½ tsp (2.5ml) hot pepper sauce
4 slices streaky bacon
1 tbsp (15ml) oil

(continued opposite)

(Jambalaya continued)

4 oz (100g) long grain rice
4 sprigs fresh thyme OR 1 tbsp (15ml) freeze-dried
8.1 oz (230g) can chopped tomatoes
Salt and freshly milled pepper
4 oz (100g) fresh cooked peeled or canned prawns
4 oz (100g) sliced ham

1. Peel and thinly slice the onion. Peel and crush the garlic and add to the onion. Slice the pepper, discarding the stem, seeds and pith. Set aside.
2. Dissolve the stock cube in the water and add the pepper sauce. (If you like really peppery-hot food add more sauce at the end of the cooking time.)
3. Cut the bacon into 1 in/2.5cm pieces, discarding any rinds. Place in the frypan and cook over medium-high heat, stirring constantly, until crisp and brown. Remove with a slotted spoon and keep hot.
4. Add the oil to the bacon fat in the pan and stir in the onion and garlic. Cook, stirring, until just soft. Add the green pepper and cook for a minute or two longer.
5. Add the rice, stirring well to coat with the oil. Add the stock, thyme and tomatoes. Bring just to the boil. Cover, reduce the heat to a gentle simmer and cook for 10–12 mins., stirring once or twice, until the rice is just tender.
6. Season to taste. Gently stir in the prawns (drain if using canned). Coarsely chop the ham and add to the pan. Cook for 2–3 mins. or until heated through. Serve immediately, spooned onto hot plates and sprinkled with the crisp bacon.

RICE A LA GREQUE
Serves two   *Takes approx. 20 mins.*

Tender plump grains of rice, simmered in stock and white
wine and then tossed with cubes of crumbly, salty Greek
Feta cheese, black olives and chopped mint.

Serve the Rice with sliced ripe tomatoes sprinkled with
a little sugar, salt and pepper plus lots of crusty warm
bread. It is also superb served with large grilled or
barbecued prawns in their shells.

1 small onion
1 vegetable stock cube
½ pt (300ml) boiling water
¼ pt (150ml) dry white vermouth
1 tbsp (15ml) olive oil
6 oz (175g) Arborio OR long grain rice
6 oz (175g) Feta cheese
3 oz (75g) large black olives
2 tbsp (30ml) chopped fresh mint
Freshly milled black pepper
2 lemon wedges

1. Peel and finely chop the onion. Dissolve the stock
    cube in the boiling water and add the vermouth.
2. Heat the oil in the frypan and stir in the onion. Cook,
    stirring, over medium heat until just soft but not
    brown.
3. Stir in the rice and cook, stirring, for 1 min. Stir in the
    stock/vermouth and bring just to the boil. Cover,
    reduce the heat and gently simmer until the rice is just
    tender, about 10 mins.
4. Meanwhile, cut the cheese into ¾ in/2cm cubes.
5. Stir the cheese, olives and mint into the fully cooked
    rice and season with pepper (the cheese is salty so you
    won't need to add extra salt). Serve immediately,
    garnished with the lemon wedges.

BACON AND LEEK PILAFF
Serves two   *Takes approx. 25 mins.*

Cooking the bacon pieces first and only returning them to the pan just before serving keeps them crisp. For a softer result, leave in the pan for the whole cooking time. No leeks? This dish is just as good using extra onions instead.

Serve the Pilaff with crisp mixed salad greens lightly tossed with oil and vinegar dressing.

8 oz (225g) leeks
1 small onion
1 clove garlic
1 chicken or vegetable stock cube
½ pt (300ml) boiling water
8 oz (225g) streaky bacon
1 tbsp (15ml) oil
4 oz (100g) long grain rice
2 oz (50g) Caerphilly or Cheddar cheese

1. Trim and clean the leeks. Cut into 1 in/2.5cm slices. Set aside. Peel and thinly slice the onion, peel and crush the garlic clove and add both to the leeks.
2. Crumble the stock cube into the water, stir to dissolve.
3. Remove any bacon rinds and cut across into 1 in/2.5cm pieces.
4. Heat the oil in the frypan and cook the bacon, stirring, until crisp. Remove with a slotted spoon onto paper towel. Set aside.
5. Add the leeks, onion and garlic to the pan and cook, stirring, until soft. Stir in the rice and continue to cook for 2 mins.
6. Stir in the stock and bring just to the boil. Reduce the heat, cover and gently simmer for 10–15 mins. or until the rice is tender. Meanwhile grate the cheese.
7. Fold in the bacon pieces and spoon onto hot serving plates. Serve immediately topped with the grated cheese.

STIR FRIED RICE
Serves two   *Takes approx. 8 mins.*

Just the recipe for when you are very hungry but short on
time. The ingredients can be varied – instead of ham use
cooked poultry, canned tuna or sliced cooked sausages
such as Frankfurters; mushrooms, courgettes or broccoli
taste just as good as beans. Cans of cooked rice are good
store cupboard stand-bys or use cooked rice left over
from a previous meal.
   Serve with crusty bread and a sliced tomato salad.

4 oz (100g) young whole green beans
6 spring onions
4 oz (100g) sliced ham
1 egg
1 tbsp (15ml) cold water
Salt and freshly milled pepper
1 oz (15g) butter
227g can fully cooked long grain rice
Soy sauce

1. 'Top and tail' the green beans and cut diagonally into
    1 in/2.5cm slices. Trim the spring onions and cut into
    the same-sized slices. Set aside.
2. Roll up the ham and cut across into thin ribbons.
3. Beat the egg and water together with a fork. Season.
4. Heat one quarter of the butter in the frypan. Pour in
    the egg. Cook over medium heat until just set, gently
    lifting the edges as they set, to allow uncooked egg to
    run underneath. Carefully roll up the egg (like a Swiss
    roll) and slide onto a hot plate. Keep warm.
5. Heat the remaining butter and stir in the beans and
    onions. Cook over high heat, stirring constantly, for 2
    mins. Add the rice and continue to cook, stirring, for
    2–3 mins. until piping hot.
6. Slice the egg roll into ribbons like the ham and add
    both to the pan. Very gently mix into the rice then pile
    onto hot plates and serve immediately, sprinkling with
    a little soy sauce if wished.

HAM AND BANANA RICE

Serves two   *Takes approx. 20 mins.*

A very simple rice dish with a tropical twist! Ham steaks, corn and slices of banana topped with salted peanuts. Choose thick bacon chops as they remain moist when cooked.

Stay with the tropical theme and serve with a sharp-flavoured salad of orange and grapefruit segments arranged on lettuce leaves and sprinkled with a little oil and vinegar dressing.

1 medium onion
1 clove garlic
2 thick-cut bacon chops – about 5 oz (150g) each
1 tsp (5ml) oil
4 oz (100g) long grain rice
7 oz (198g) can corn kernels
1 vegetable stock cube
½ pt (300ml) boiling water
Freshly milled pepper
1 large banana
2 oz (50g) salted peanuts

1. Peel and thinly slice the onion. Peel and crush the garlic clove. Add to the onion and set aside.
2. Cut the fat of the bacon chops two or three times (at right angles to the edge). This avoids the chops curling up as they cook.
3. Heat the oil in the frypan, add the chops and cook over medium-high heat until golden brown. Turn them several times, pressing them down onto the surface of the pan. Remove from the pan with a fork and keep hot.
4. Add the onion and garlic to the hot pan and cook, stirring frequently, until just beginning to brown. Stir in the rice and cook for a further 2 mins.
5. Add the undrained corn, crumble the stock cube over and add the boiling water. Stir well, cover and cook over gentle heat until the rice is just cooked – about 8 mins. Season with pepper.
6. Thickly slice the banana and stir in.
7. Serve the bacon chops with the rice, sprinkling the nuts on top.

CHICKEN RISOTTO MONTEREY
Serves two   *Takes approx. 25 mins.*

Another delicious example of the Californian knack of combining fruits with savoury ingredients. Meaty chicken thighs gently simmer with the rice then have a citrus-flavoured cream spooned over, which the rice absorbs. The garnish of orange and lemon segments adds a fresh-tasting contrast.

Another fruit grown in California is the kiwi. Carefully peel off the hairy brown skin, cut into wedges and add to a mixed green salad lightly tossed with an oil and vinegar dressing. Top with some Californian walnut halves and serve with the Risotto.

1 lemon
1 orange
4 tbsp (60ml) double cream
1 chicken stock cube
½ pt (300ml) boiling water
6 spring onions
1 oz (25g) flaked almonds
1 tbsp (15ml) olive oil
4 large chicken thighs (skinned if wished)
4 oz (100g) long grain rice
Salt and freshly milled pepper

1. Finely grate the rind from half of the lemon and half the orange. Add to the cream, stir and set aside.
2. Using a small sharp knife, remove the remaining rind and white pith from both the fruits. Holding each fruit in the palm of your hand, carefully slice between the membrane to cut out the fruit segments, allowing them to drop onto a plate. Set aside.
3. Dissolve the stock cube in the boiling water.
4. Trim the spring onions and cut into 1 in/2.5cm pieces.
5. Sprinkle the almonds in the frypan and cook over medium-high heat until golden brown, stirring constantly. Tip out onto paper towel. Set aside.
6. Heat the oil in the frypan and add the chicken thighs. Cook over medium-high heat, turning frequently, until brown on all sides.

7. Remove the pan from the heat and add the spring onions, rice and stock to the pan. Stir to moisten all the rice.
8. Return the pan to the heat and bring just to the boil.
9. Cover, reduce the heat to medium-low and simmer until the chicken is tender and cooked through – about 20 mins. The rice should also be tender and have absorbed the stock. (If cooked too fast, the rice will have absorbed all the stock before it is tender. If this happens, add a little more hot water to the pan and reduce the heat.)
10. Spoon the cream over and cook a minute or two longer until bubbling hot. Season to taste.
11. Arrange the orange and lemon segments to one side of warm serving plates. Add the rice and chicken and sprinkle with the almonds. Serve immediately.

PERSIAN PILAFF
Serves two   *Takes approx. 20 mins.*

Golden rice studded with fruits and nuts – a very simple rice dish bursting with colour and flavour. Saffron is the dried stigmas of a crocus which takes its name from Saffron Walden, Essex. Now imported from Spain, it is very expensive but a tiny pinch goes a long way. Turmeric can be used instead, but the flavour and colour will not be the same.

The Pilaff is very satisfying on its own or I like to serve it with cold ham or chicken, and sliced avocados, plus hot rolls.

2 oz (50g) whole blanched almonds
1 medium onion
1 large orange
1 chicken stock cube
¾ pt (450ml) boiling water
4 oz (100g) ready-to-eat dried apricots
1 oz (25g) butter

(continued overleaf)

(Persian Pilaff continued)

Pinch of saffron
4 oz (100g) Basmati rice
2 oz (50g) sultanas

1. Cut each almond in half lengthwise – into tiny 'chips'. Peel and thinly slice the onion. Finely grate the orange peel. Using a small, sharp knife carefully cut off all the remaining peel and pith. Hold the orange in the palm of your hand and carefully cut out each wedge of flesh, allowing it to drop onto a plate. Set aside.
2. Dissolve the chicken stock cube in the hot water. Cut the apricots in half. Set aside.
3. Melt half the butter in the frypan and toss in the almonds. Cook, stirring constantly, over medium-high heat until golden brown. Remove with a slotted spoon onto paper towel.
4. Add the remaining butter to the pan and stir in the onion. Cook, stirring, until soft and pale golden brown. Stir in saffron and rice and continue to cook for 2 mins.
5. Add the grated orange peel, the apricots, sultanas and stock. Bring just to the boil.
6. Cover, reduce the heat to a very gentle simmer and cook for 12–15 mins. or until the rice is tender and has absorbed the stock.
7. Gently fold in the almonds and orange segments. Spoon onto hot plates and serve immediately.

RED BEANS AND RICE
Serves two   *Takes approx. 18 mins.*

Find some really meaty sausages with added spices or herbs for this recipe; perhaps your local butcher makes up his own special recipe? Alternatively use the spicy Spanish Chorizo or the Italian Pepperoni sausage. The dry red wine adds to the flavour but the recipe is still very good without it. (Use extra boiling water instead.)

Serve Red Beans and Rice with hot granary bread, celery sticks and crisp radishes.

1 medium onion
2 young carrots
2 sticks celery
1 vegetable stock cube
10 fl oz (300ml) boiling water
2 fl oz (50ml) dry red wine
8 oz (225g) sausages
2 tsp (10ml) oil
4 oz (100g) long grain rice
2 tsp (10ml) fennel seeds
Salt and freshly milled pepper
7.5 oz (213g) can kidney beans, drained

1. Peel and finely chop the onion. Scrub or peel the carrots and cut into small dice. Add to the onion. Thinly slice the celery, reserving any leaves for garnish. Set aside. Dissolve the stock cube in the water and add the wine.
2. Skin the sausages and cut into 1 in/2.5cm slices. (Cut the drier smoked Chorizos or Pepperoni into ½ in/1.25cm slices.)
3. Heat the oil in the frypan and add the sausages. Cook over medium heat, stirring frequently, until golden brown. Remove from the pan with a slotted spoon and keep hot.
4. Add the onion and carrot to the pan. Cook, stirring, over medium-high heat until the onion is soft. Add the celery and rice, stirring to coat with the oil.
5. Stir in the stock/wine and the fennel seeds and bring just to the boil. Cover, reduce the heat and gently simmer until the rice is just tender – about 10 mins. Season to taste.
6. Return the sausages to the pan with the beans and continue to cook until bubbling hot. Serve immediately, garnished with the celery leaves.

COURGETTE AND BLUE CHEESE RISOTTO
Serves two   *Takes approx. 20 mins.*

Choose your favourite blue cheese for this recipe from the very wide variety now available. Button mushrooms or broccoli may be used in place of the courgettes, and long grain rice instead of Arborio.

Serve the rich-flavoured Risotto with a salad of watercress and grapefruit segments lightly sprinkled with oil and vinegar dressing.

8 oz (225g) young courgettes
1 small onion
4 oz (100g) blue cheese
1 chicken stock cube
½ pt (300ml) boiling water
¼ pt (150ml) dry white wine
1 oz (25g) pinenuts
1 tbsp (15ml) olive oil
6 oz (175g) Arborio rice
Freshly milled pepper

1. Trim the courgettes and cut into small chunks. Peel and finely chop the onion. Grate or crumble the cheese. Dissolve the stock cube in the water and add the wine. Set aside.
2. Sprinkle the pinenuts in the frypan and cook, without any oil, until golden brown, stirring constantly. Tip onto paper towel.
3. Heat half the oil in the frypan and add the courgettes. Cook over medium-high heat until just golden brown and still quite crisp. Remove from the pan with a slotted spoon and keep hot.
4. Add remaining oil to the pan and stir in the onion. Cook, stirring, until just soft but not brown. Stir in the rice and cook for a further minute.
5. Add the stock/wine and bring just to the boil. Cover, reduce the heat and gently simmer until the rice is just tender, about 10 mins.
6. Add the cheese and stir until just beginning to melt. Season to taste with pepper. Gently stir in the courgettes.
7. Spoon onto hot plates and sprinkle with the toasted pinenuts. Serve immediately.

TUNA RISOTTO
Serves two *Takes approx. 15 mins.*

The large round-grained rice called Arborio is the traditional choice for a risotto and may be found in most supermarkets or Italian delicatessens. If not to hand use long grain rice. The mild flavour of leeks goes well with the fish but a small onion could be used instead.

Serve the Risotto with a salad of crunchy iceberg lettuce and diced green-skinned eating apple (leave the skin on) tossed with a little oil and vinegar dressing.

2 medium leeks
8 oz (225g) small courgettes
1 lemon
½ oz (15g) butter
1 oz (25g) flaked almonds
1 vegetable stock cube
¼ pt (150ml) boiling water
4 oz (100g) Arborio rice
7 oz (198g) can tuna in brine
Freshly milled black pepper

1. Trim and clean the leeks. Cut into 1 in/2.5cm slices. Set aside. Trim the courgettes and also cut into 1 in/ 2.5cm slices. Add to the leeks. Finely grate the rind of the lemon and remove the juice. Set aside.
2. Heat the butter in the frypan, sprinkle in the almonds and cook over medium heat, stirring constantly, until golden brown. Tip onto paper towel.
3. Tip the leeks and courgettes into the pan, increase the heat and cook, stirring, until they begin to brown.
4. Crumble the stock cube over and add the boiling water, the lemon rind and juice. Sprinkle the rice over and stir well. Bring just to the boil, reduce the heat to a very gentle simmer and cover.
5. Simmer for 10 mins. or until the rice is just tender. (If the rice cooks too fast, it will absorb all the stock before it is tender; so stir in a little extra boiling water and lower the heat.)
6. Meanwhile, drain the tuna and break into chunks.
7. Season the risotto with pepper and gently fold in the fish. Serve immediately, topped with the almonds.

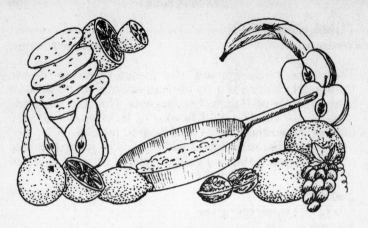

12. SWEET ENDINGS

RICH KNIGHTS OF WINDSOR

Serves two   *Takes approx. 8 mins.*

This is my version of a traditional recipe called the Poor Knights of Windsor. It seems those impoverished gentlemen had to make do with the dessert made with white bread. Today we are spoilt for choice at the bakery so I have used the slightly sweet rich brioche bread.

A spoonful of chilled Cornish clotted cream would elevate this dish to the Very Rich Knights of Windsor!

¼ pt (150ml) milk
1 tbsp (15ml) sugar
1 tbsp (15ml) sweet sherry
1 egg yolk
2 thick slices cut from a brioche loaf
1 oz (25g) butter

1. Whisk the milk with the sugar, sherry and egg yolk in a large, shallow plate.
2. Add the brioche slices and turn them over. Leave for a minute or two until they have absorbed the milk mixture.
3. Heat the butter in the frypan and slide in the brioche.
4. Cook over medium-high heat until golden brown on both sides, turning gently to avoid breaking the bread.
5. Serve immediately.

BLUSHING PEARS

Serves two   *Takes approx. 6 mins.*

Juicy pear slices in a rosy pink cream sauce. Serve with Italian Amaretti biscuits – almond cushions wrapped like Christmas crackers each in their own crisp tissue paper.

2 large dessert pears
½ oz (15ml) butter
3 tbsp (45ml) redcurrant jelly
1 tbsp (15ml) lemon juice
3 fl oz (75ml) double cream

1. Peel and halve the pears. Scoop out and discard the core and cut fruit into thick slices.
2. Melt the butter in the frypan and slip in the pear slices.
3. Cook over medium-high heat until soft and beginning to brown on both sides – about 3 mins. Be careful not to break the fruit when turning it over.
4. Arrange the pear slices on warm serving plates and keep hot.
5. Add the redcurrant jelly and lemon juice to the pan and stir until melted. Blend in the cream and heat just until bubbling hot.
6. Spoon over the pears and serve immediately.

HOT FRUIT SALAD
Serves two   *Takes approx. 8 mins.*

A new twist to the familiar fruit dessert. The kinds of fruit
used can be varied but make sure you have at least one
grapefruit or orange to flavour the syrup.
  Serve bubbling hot, with cream or Greek yoghurt.

1 pink grapefruit
1 white grapefruit
1 orange
1 eating apple
1 small banana
4 oz (100g) granulated sugar
Cold water

1. Using a small, sharp knife carefully cut off the skin of
    both grapefruit and the orange. This can be done two
    ways. Either cut round the fruit making one long strip
    of peel. Or cut a slice from each end, stand one of
    the cut ends on the work surface and cut down in thin
    strips like the staves of a barrel. Cut away any
    remaining pith.
2. Holding the fruit in one hand and over a plate to catch
    the juices, cut out each wedge of flesh, allowing it to
    drop onto the plate. Squeeze the pulp left in your
    hand to extract any juice then discard the pulp.
    Repeat with the other citrus fruit.
3. Cut the apple into thin slices, discarding the core but
    not peeling first. Peel and slice the banana.
4. Carefully drain the citrus fruit juice into a measuring
    jug and make up to 6 fl oz (175ml) with cold water.
5. Place the sugar and water in the frypan. Over medium
    heat, stir constantly until the sugar has melted.
    Increase the heat and boil for 3–4 mins. or until
    syrupy.
6. Add the fruit and cook, stirring, until bubbling hot
    and the apple and banana are translucent. Serve
    immediately.

CINNAMON TOASTS WITH LEMON SWIRL YOGHURT

Serves two   *Takes approx. 6 mins.*

Crisp fingers of spiced French toast with cool creamy lemon-flavoured yoghurt.

¼ pt (150ml) Greek yoghurt
2 tbsp (30ml) lemon curd
¼ pt (150ml) milk
1 egg
2 thick slices fresh bread
1 oz (25g) butter
2 tbsp (30ml) demerara sugar
¼ tsp (1.25ml) ground cinnamon

1. Spoon the yoghurt into a medium-sized bowl and drizzle the lemon curd over. Using a wire whisk or a fork, lightly swirl the lemon curd through the yoghurt – just until it looks 'marbled'. Chill in the fridge.
2. Whisk together the milk and egg in a large, shallow plate.
3. Trim the crusts from the bread and slide the bread into the milk mixture. Turn the bread over and leave to soak for a minute or two to absorb the milk mixture.
4. Heat the butter in the frypan and add the bread slices. Cook over medium-high heat until golden brown on both sides. Turn carefully to avoid breaking the bread.
5. Cut each slice into three and arrange on warm serving plates.
6. Combine the sugar and cinnamon and sprinkle over the toasts. Serve immediately with the lemon yoghurt.

GOLDEN APPLE RINGS WITH CINNAMON CRUMBS

Serves two   *Takes approx. 8 mins.*

Poaching apple rings in orange juice gives them a beautiful golden glow. You could use freshly squeezed juice but the unsweetened variety from a carton is just as good.

Top with the crisp spiced crumbs and serve piping hot with a cool spoonful of fromage frais or Greek yoghurt.

2 slices fresh bread
3 tbsp (45ml) demerara sugar
¼ tsp (1.25ml) ground cinnamon
2 large eating apples
1 oz (25g) butter
¼ pt (150ml) orange juice

1. Trim the crusts off the bread and make into crumbs – in a processor or using a grater. Mix with the sugar and spice.
2. Peel and core the apples with an apple corer. Cut each across into four or five slices to form rings.
3. Melt the butter in the frypan and stir in the crumbs, sugar and cinnamon mixture.
4. Cook over medium-high heat until a rich golden brown. Stir constantly as the crumbs will quickly burn. Tip onto a plate.
5. Carefully wipe the pan with paper towel.
6. Pour the orange juice into the pan and add the apple rings. Cover and cook over medium heat until soft and translucent – about 4 mins. Turn the rings over several times during cooking.
7. Arrange the apple rings on warm plates, sprinkle with the crumbs and serve immediately.

BUTTERSCOTCH PANCAKES
Serves two *Takes approx. 3 mins.*

Ready-made Scotch pancakes are sold in the bakery section of supermarkets. Heated through in a spiced butterscotch sauce they are very 'more-ish', especially when served topped with well chilled Cornish clotted cream!

Use four to six pancakes, depending on their size – and your appetite!

½ oz (15g) butter
2 tbsp (30ml) soft dark brown sugar
1 tsp (5ml) ground cinnamon
2 tbsp (30ml) orange juice
4–6 Scotch pancakes

1. Melt the butter in the frypan over medium-high heat. Stir in the sugar and cinnamon.
2. Continue to cook, stirring until the sugar has melted.
3. Stir in the orange juice and heat until bubbling, about 30 seconds.
4. Add the pancakes, turning to coat with the sauce. Cook, turning frequently, until very hot, about 1½ mins.
5. Serve immediately.

LEMON AND APPLE PANCAKES
Serves two   *Takes approx. 5 mins.*

First poach apple slices in a sharp lemon syrup until tender then add Scotch pancakes and cook until bubbling hot.
    Serve with a scoop of vanilla ice-cream.

1 large lemon
1 eating apple
2 fl oz (50ml) cold water
3 oz (75g) sugar
4–6 Scotch pancakes

1. Finely grate the lemon rind and extract the juice from the lemon. Peel the apple, remove the core with an apple corer and cut across into 4–6 slices.
2. Place the lemon rind, juice, water and sugar in the frypan.
3. Cook over medium-high heat, stirring constantly, until the sugar has melted and the liquid has reduced and become syrupy, about 2 mins.
4. Add the apple slices, turning to coat with the syrup. Cook, turning gently, until soft and translucent. Using a slotted spoon, lift the apple slices onto two warm plates and keep hot.
5. Add the pancakes to the pan. Cook, turning once or twice, until very hot, about 1½ mins. Add to the apple slices, spooning over the syrup. Serve immediately.

TANGY ORANGE PANCAKES

Serves two   *Takes approx. 5 mins.*

Another delicious dessert using the ready-made Scotch pancakes found in all bakeries and supermarket bakery departments.

A spoonful of Greek yoghurt adds that final touch!

2 large oranges
4 tbsp (60ml) fine-cut marmalade
4–6 Scotch pancakes

1. Squeeze the juice from one orange. Peel and cut out the segments from the other (see Hot Fruit Salad, page 148, for method).
2. Place the juice and marmalade in the frypan.
3. Gently warm over medium-high heat, stirring, until the marmalade has melted – about 1 min.
4. Add the pancakes, turning them to coat with the sauce. Cook, turning frequently, until very hot – about 1½ mins.
5. Tuck the orange segments around the pancakes and cook a minute longer to heat them through.
6. Serve immediately, spooning the oranges and sauce over the pancakes.

BANANAS WITH RUM
Serves two   *Takes approx. 5 mins.*

Serve spooned over ice-cream, preferably coffee-flavoured.

2 oz (50g) butter
1 oz (25g) walnut halves
2 oz (50g) soft brown sugar
Pinch cinnamon
2 fl oz (50ml) cold water
2 tbsp (30ml) dark rum
2 large bananas

1. Melt a quarter of the butter in the frypan, add the walnuts and cook, stirring constantly, over high heat until golden brown. Remove with a slotted spoon.
2. Add the remaining butter, the sugar and cinnamon to the pan. Cook over medium heat, stirring constantly, until melted.
3. Off the heat, very slowly pour the water into the pan. (It may spit.) Add the rum. Return to the heat and bring to the boil.
4. Peel and thickly slice the fruit. Add to the pan and continue to cook, stirring, until the fruit becomes translucent and the sauce has thickened. Serve immediately sprinkled with the walnuts.

INDEX

RIGHT WAY
PUBLISHING POLICY

HOW WE SELECT TITLES
RIGHT WAY consider carefully every deserving manuscript. Where an author is an authority on his subject but an inexperienced writer, we provide first-class editorial help. The standards we set make sure that every **RIGHT WAY** book is practical, easy to understand, concise, informative and delightful to read. Our specialist artists are skilled at creating simple illustrations which augment the text wherever necessary.

CONSISTENT QUALITY
At every reprint our books are updated where appropriate, giving our authors the opportunity to include new information.

FAST DELIVERY
We sell **RIGHT WAY** books to the best bookshops throughout the world. It may be that your bookseller has run out of stock of a particular title. If so, he can order more from us at any time – we have a fine reputation for "same day" despatch, and we supply any order, however small (even a single copy), to any bookseller who has an account with us. We prefer you to buy from your bookseller, as this reminds him of the strong underlying public demand for **RIGHT WAY** books. Readers who live in remote places, or who are house-bound, or whose local bookseller is unco-operative, can order direct from us by post.

FREE
If you would like an up-to-date list of all **RIGHT WAY** titles currently available, send a stamped self-addressed envelope to
ELLIOT RIGHT WAY BOOKS, BRIGHTON ROAD,
LOWER KINGSWOOD, TADWORTH, SURREY, KT20 6TD,U.K.
or visit our web site at www.right-way.co.uk